ISHTUR PHAKDE

ISHTUR PHAKDE:
A GALLANT ENGLISHMAN AND OTHER STUDIES

C. A. KINCAID

GYAN

Published by

Gyan Publishing House
5, Ansari Road
Daryaganj, New Delhi-110002
Phone: 011-47034999, 9811692060
E-mail: books@gyanbooks.com

Distribution Network
gyanbooks.com
India, USA, Canada, UK, Australia

ISBN: 978-93-7014-033-2 (PB)

First Published, 1917

2nd Impression 2025

Printed at: Gyan Press, Delhi.

ISHTUR PHAKDE:
A GALLANT ENGLISHMAN AND OTHER STUDIES
Author: C. A. KINCAID

ISHTUR PHAKDE

A GALLANT ENGLISHMAN

AND OTHER STUDIES

BY

C. A. KINCAID, C.V.O., I.C.S.

Author of The Indian Heroes; Deccan Nursery Tales the Tale of the Tulsi Plant; the Outlaws of Kathiawar.

BOMBAY

THE TIMES PRESS

1917

PREFACE

With two exceptions the following studies appeared in *The Times of India*. I am indebted to the editor for permission to reprint them.

C. A. K.

To

MY MOTHER

CONTENTS

I.

"ISHTUR PHAKDE."

A GALLANT ENGLISHMAN.

IN the days both of the Maratha and Chitpavan rulers rewards and titles for valour and for generalship were, as is the case in all military governments, neither few nor lacking in variety. There were Senapatis and Senakhas Khels, Shamsher Bahadurs and Hambirraos, Zunjarraos and Rustamraos, Hinduraos and Jaysingraos. But there was one title never bestowed by any Maratha Government but by the universal judgment of the army. And so high were the qualities which could deserve it, that in the two centuries of Maratha history only three persons were considered fit for it. The title was that of 'Phakde,' a word almost impossible to translate accurately into English. To earn the title it was not sufficient to be recklessly daring. One had also to possess qualities which the French describe in the word *preux* and the Italians in the phrase *galantuomo*. One had in fact to combine in one person the chivalry of a Bayard, the fortitude of a Sydney and the headlong bravery of a Marshal Ney.

The first of these three persons was one Kanherrao Trimbak Ekbote. He appears to have begun his military service as a common trooper about the time that Balaji Bajirao succeeded his father as Peshwa. It was not long before he rose to a Captain's command. But it was in the arduous campaign of 1751-1752 that he earned the title of Phakde. The Marathas had long hoped that sooner or later the kingdom, founded by the Nizam-ul-Mulk from the ruins of the Deccan province of the Moguls, would fall like a ripe fruit into their mouths. And this desirable conclusion would no doubt have occurred, but for an event which no human ingenuity could have anticipated. This event was the arrival of M. De Bussy in India. This admirable soldier was a Marquis in his own country. But poverty and a love of adventure had driven him to seek his fortunes in the East. There his eminent talents soon attracted the notice of Dupleix and he was sent by him to support Salabat Jang, one of the several sons of the Nizam-ul-Mulk, who were then struggling with each other to secure his inheritance. Aided by De Bussy, Salabat Jang soon disposed of his rivals and in 1751 turned the tables on the victorious Marathas by marching on Poona. At Rajapur on the Ghod river, De Bussy, taking advantage of an eclipse, surprised the Marathas while engaged in their religious devotions and completely dispersed their army. The Marathas, however, rallied and on 27th November 1751 attacked the Moguls with such determination, that nothing but the French artillery saved them from defeat. By general consent the most gallant of the attacking force was Kanherrao Ekbote. As a reward from the Peshwa he obtained the right of wearing a silver bangle on his horse's foreleg. From the common soldiery he obtained a still higher honour. For from that day onwards he was known by them as Kanherrao Phakde. In the end M. De Bussy and the Moguls, weary of war, retreated to Hyderabad.

But five years later the French general had his revenge. Kanherrao Phakde's cavalry again met the French artillery in Savanut. The Maratha leader charged the guns with his accustomed daring. But in midcharge a French cannon ball struck him on the head and the gallant cavalry leader fell never to rise again.

The second of the three Phakdes was one Manaji Shinde. He bore the same name as the founder of the Shinde principality. But whereas Mahadji Shinde was the illegitimate member of a younger branch of the family, Manaji Shinde was the legitimate heir of the eldest branch. This circumstance, as well as Manaji's high military reputation, all but induced the elder Madhavrao to name him as heir to Ranoji Shinde's Jaghir. Had Madhavrao done so, the history of India would have had to be differently written. But in the end justice prevailed. And Mahadji Shinde was appointed to succeed his father. Manaji Shinde was a faithful follower of Raghunathrao Peshwa, and his fortunes sank with those of that pretender. He was eventually reconciled to Nana Phadnavis. But he sullied his fame and title by deserting to Haider Ali in 1778. His reputation, however, for bravery was such that it was almost as great in the Bombay as in the Poona army. In 1791 a Darbar was held in Poona to celebrate the treaty of alliance between the Marathas and the English. Sir Charles Malet was the English plenipotentiary and among his suite was one Major Price, who has left an interesting record of the ceremonial. In it occurs the following passage:—"Among others was Manaji Fankra (Phakde) long known to the Bombay army for his reckless bravery. His grotesque appearance, on the present occasion, was peculiarly striking. . . . His face, heart and arms were so strangely painted in streaks of yellow, as might have taken the conceit out of the wildest of the red chiefs of the American wilderness, and certainly, when leaning on his shield with a settled scowl upon his countenance, he exhibited an exterior of savage ferocity, whatever might have been the animating spirit." Another Englishman, Tone by name, described Manaji Phakde two years later as "an officer of high military reputation and so disfigured with wounds, as to have scarcely the appearance of a human creature."

The third of this remarkable trio was an Englishman. His name was Captain James Stewart, and his story so far as is known of him is briefly as follows :—

In the year 1773 the Peshwa Narainrao had been murdered with the connivance, if not under the orders, of his uncle Raghunathrao. The latter, on his nephew's death, seized the Government. But the fruits of his crime were snatched from him by the skill and resource of Nana Phadnavis. The Minister, taking advantage of Raghunathrao's absence in camp, successfully proclaimed Narainrao's infant son as ruler. Raghunathrao fled to the English at Bombay. There the Government, with very little knowledge of the question before them, espoused the fugitive's cause. They first conducted with some success a campaign in Gujarat, until their action was overruled by the supreme Government at Bengal. Then, interpreting a despatch from Calcutta which empowered them to 'tranquillize' the dissensions of the Maratha state as authorising them to make war, the Bombay Government formed the design of marching on Poona itself and of installing Raghunathrao by armed force. The army to which the Government entrusted this considerable task consisted all told only of 3,900 men. But such was the prestige of one of its officers that, had he survived, the object of the tiny army would probably have been attained. The officer in question was one Captain James Stewart. I have not been able to trace the earlier history of this remarkable man. But such had been his gallantry in the field that the title of Phakde had been conferred on him by his own men while he still had only a subaltern's rank. And the justice of his claim to it was established by the instant acceptance of the title by the Peshwa's army and the Peshwa's Government. Indeed when the British force started to place Raghunathrao on the throne, the name of "Ishtur Phakde" was as well-known in Poona as in Bombay and his mere presence in the hostile force was sufficient to inspire the Poona Government with the darkest forebodings. Captain Stewart was appointed by Colonel Egerton, the General Commanding, to lead the advance guard. He acted up to his high reputation and on the 22nd November 1778, he with six companies of sepoys and some light artillery surprised the Bhor Ghat and encamped at Khandala before the Maratha army realised that he was on the move. For the next month he was exposed to constant attacks from the Maratha cavalry. Nevertheless such was the effect of his name alike on his own and on the enemy's force, that he successfully held the pass until the entire British force had joined him. The army then set out for Poona and the whole brunt of the attack was met by Captain Stewart whose advance guard drove back the enemy with the utmost spirit. Unfortunately he had no longer the command of the invading force and its progress under Colonel Egerton was much too slow. Nevertheless all went well until the 4th January 1779, when the Bombay army reached Karla, a village only eight miles from the spot which Captain Stewart had occupied six weeks before. The creeping advance of the Bombay army had given the Marathas time to collect an army large enough to create even in Captain Stewart some misgivings. According to the Maratha account he climbed a tree in order to reconnoitre the enemy's position. His commanding figure, however, was at once recognised and the entire Maratha front resounded with the cry of "Shabash, Ishtur Phakde." At the same time Haripant Tatya who commanded the Maratha artillery aimed a number of guns upon the tree which sheltered Stewart. A moment later the tree and its burden were swept away in a storm of cannon shot. As Stewart fell dead at Karla, a strange incident happened at Poona. The news which had so far reached the Peshwa's Court was far from reassuring and the boy prince's household were a prey to despondency. Suddenly Madhavrao II rose to his feet and asked them the cause of their gloom. "The English," they replied, "will not give way." The boy prince sent for his sword, fastened it on and then said "The Englishman is dead." To his listeners there was only one Englishman who mattered. And the same evening a breathless rider brought the news that "Ishtur Phakde" was no more. By some mysterious telepathy the death of the English hero had reached the Brahman prince several hours before the galloping messenger. The Maratha hopes raised by this news were shortly afterwards fulfilled. Within nine days of Stewart's death the English army, after an unsuccessful effort to retreat, surrendered at Wadgaon, some 20 miles from Poona.

No tomb-stone marks the grave where Stewart lies. The Encyclopædia Britannica knows him not. Yet he has obtained a more enduring monument than sculptured stone or written page. Bengali mothers may still, as when Macaulay wrote, croon to their babies jingling ditties of Warren Hastings and his caparisoned elephants. The name of Nicholson still looms large among the Punjab Sikhs. Yet for Warren Hastings or for Nicholson the Poona public care nothing. But to-day the legend of "Isthur Phakde" is as fresh among the Deshasth and Chitpavan Brahmans of Poona as when he fell, swept away by Hari Tatya's batteries. Something indeed Stewart owes to the circumstances which followed his end. Had the force which his courage inspired been victorious, his memory would probably have passed away like that of Clive or Wellesley. But his fall is associated in Maratha minds with their greatest victory over their English conquerors. He was the Ravana of a modern Ramayana, the Hector of a Marathi Iliad. Nevertheless, honour to the man whose fame a century has failed to dim. And honour too, to the chivalry of a race, who have gathered a foreigner and an enemy into the Valhalla of their heroes.

II.

THE MAKAR SANKRANT.

"WHAT is the Makar Sankrant?" This is a question which will probably be asked by Englishmen a good many times in the course of to-day. This is especially likely if they are Government servants and learn that to-day their office is closed. For they will naturally ask who this unknown friend with the strange name is, who has so happily intervened between them and their labours. The word Makar is literally a sea monster; but in this connection it is the sign of the Zodiac corresponding with Capricorn. Sankrant means the crossing and the two words combined mean that the sun to-day leaves the Zodiac sign of Dhan or Sagitarius and enters that of Makar or Capricorn. High festival is held because the sun has passed the extreme southern point of the ecliptic and begins to move in a northerly direction towards the equator. In other words, the Makar Sankrant is the winter solstice, and the Hindus who once lived in a northern climate and knew the bitterness of the long winter nights celebrate to-day the future increase of the daylight. But the objection naturally arises that to-day is not the shortest day and that the winter solstice falls on the 21st to the 23rd December. Now what is the cause of this difference? It requires some explanation not over easy to one not learned in astronomy. However here goes.

The ancient Hindu astronomers seem to have divided the sun's path in the heavens into 27 nakshatras, marking these divisions by the great fixed stars called by Professor Max Muller the milestones of heaven. Subsequent to their contact with Hellenism, they borrowed from the west the Zodiacal signs which they called Rashi. And like the Greeks they took the vernal equinox as the beginning of the year. Aryabhat, who lived at the close of the 5th century A.D., discovered that the earth revolved on its axis; but none of the Hindu astronomers seems to have lit on the Copernican theory that the earth went round the sun. As they did not understand the earth's motion, they never grasped that the precession of the equinoxes, by which the position of the equinectial points make a complete revolution in the course of about 25,800 years*, was due to the shifting of the earth's axis. Nevertheless the precession itself did not escape them and they actually fixed its rate, and from time to time they quietly altered the almanac. This is clear from the death of Bhishma in the Mahabharat to which I shall again refer. He died exactly when the sun began to turn northward and the date given is Magh Shudha 8th (January 29th). Thus the winter solstice according to the almanac of that time fell 16 days later than now. The present starting point of the year was fixed by Varahmihira in the 5th century A.D. But no alterations seem to have taken place since then. However in 1,400 years a considerable change has taken place in the positions of the equinoctial points. The vernal equinox no longer falls in

* Delambre's calculation (see p. 794, Vol. II, Encyclopædia Britannica, 9th Ed.) is 25,868. More recent calculations give it at 25,730.

Aries* (Mesh) but in Pisces (Min). The winter solstice falls in Dhan (Sagitarius) instead of at the beginning of Capricorn. In other words, it falls on the 21st December instead of on the 13th January.

Now it may be supposed from this that the modern Hindu knows nothing of Astronomy and Macaulay's phrase "Astronomy which would move laughter in the girls at an English boarding house" will be at once remembered. This, however, is not the case. In the treatise of Orion, the whole question of the precession of the equinoxes is discussed. Then it will be asked why the date of the Makar Sankrant is not altered. I confess that I cannot provide a confident answer. But perhaps we may find one in our own observances. The festival of Easter Sunday is supposed to correspond with the resurrection of Christ, yet it will be seen that it never recurs on the same date for 19 successive years. The reason is that it is calculated on the Greek Solar cycle. The Greeks used Lunar months, but they rectified the yearly errors of 11 days by Meton's discovery that 235 lunar months corresponded approximately with 19 solar years. Now the Church fixes Easter on the Sunday following the 1st full moon which occurs on or after the 21st March. The dates of the full moon correspond with the Metonic Cycle, that is after the lapse of 19 years, they recur on or about the same day of the year. Consequently while they vary for every year during 19 years the 20th year will correspond

*The Indian names for the 12 signs are as follows :—Mesh (aries) ; Varishabha (taurus) ; Mithun (gemini) ; Kark (cancer) ; Sinh (leo) ; Kanya (vergo) ; Tul (libra) ; Vrischik (scorpio) ; Dhan (sagitarius) ; Makar (capricornus) ; Kumbha (aquarius) ; and Min (Pisces).

approximately with the first. It may be said that this method, if clumsy, is not very incorrect astronomically. But as a matter of fact the tables of the moon on which the calculations are made are very old and according to Professor Newcomb the date fixed for Easter Sunday is even according to the Metonic Cycle a week in error. Now this is a case where at any rate astronomical ignorance is not the determining cause. It would be perfectly easy to fix a date for Easter so that it fell yearly on the same date. It would also be quite easy to correct the moon tables. The reason why this is not done is probably the same as that which prevents the alteration of the Makar Sankrant. Religion is in the first place conservative. In the second place it would be difficult to alter the day without in a measure spoiling the charm of the festival. What would Easter be unless it fell on a Sunday? Half the joy of the Makar Sankrant festival would go if it was no longer celebrated when the sun entered Capricorn.

Having considered the astronomical aspect of the holiday let us consider its social significance. We have for this purpose to assume that it is astronomically correct and that the sun really has reached the southernmost point of the ecliptic (Krantivritt) and is turning northwards to the Equator (Vishuvritt). We have therefore entered on what is known as the Uttarayan or the six lucky months. If a man dies during the Uttarayan he goes straight to heaven. If he dies during the Dakshinayan, or the six months which intervene between the sun turning southward from the northern point of the ecliptic to the Makar Sankrant, he will find heaven's gates shut and he will have to wait outside until the winter solstice. Again in five out of six of the lucky months—Magh, Falgun, Chaitra, Vaishakh and Jestha thread and marriage ceremonies can be held, while in Margashirsh alone out of the Dakshinayan months can a couple be united. Thus to celebrate the beginning of so auspicious a period Hindu men and women alike rise early, cover themselves with sesamum oil, bathe in warm water, worship the family gods and make small presents to Brahmans of sesamum seed, money, clothes, pots and umbrellas. In the afternoon they dress in their holiday clothes and visit their friends. On entering the home they present to the head of the house a packet of sugared sesamum seed and say "Til kha tilse ya gul kha godse bola" (Eat the sesamum and come towards me little by little; eat the sugar and let your words be sweet). Now why is the sesamum particularly associated with the Makar Sankrant? It is because the smallness of the sesamum represents the tiny changes which occur in the length of the day during the early part of the Uttarayan. The day, say the Hindus, lengthens only 'til, til,' or the size of a sesamum seed.

This idea of the smallness of a sesamum seed occurs also in the proverb tile tilam pashyati, *i.e.*, he sees a palmyra tree in a sesamum or makes a mountain out of a molehill.

As a set off against over rejoicing on the Makar Sankrant the morrow is an unlucky day (a kar divas). No unkind word must be spoken for as one acts on that day, so one will act through the whole year. Everywhere there must be smiling faces, and if a mother beats her children on the day after the winter solstice she will beat them every day for twelve months; so if I were a Hindu child I should keep well out of my mother's reach. It would be no use leading her into temptation.

But no account of the Makar Sankrant can be complete without a description of the death of Bhishma. Its anniversary is no doubt celebrated on the Magh Shudha Ashtmi, but this, as I have already said, was due to the winter solstice falling on that date. Bhishma is to my mind the most delightful character in the Mahabharat. He was the son of King Shantanu of Hastinapura by the river Ganges. But his mother after the manner of wayward immortals deserted her lover. So King Shantanu sought the hand of a fisher girl Satyavati. She refused to marry him unless he promised that her children would succeed to the exclusion of Bhishma. Shantanu would not consent but Bhishma of his own accord resigned his rights and vowed himself to perpetual celibacy for fear that his children might quarrel with those of Satyavati. Satyavati then bore Shantanu two sons Dritarashtra and Pandu, and they in turn became respectively the fathers of the Kauravas and the Pandavas.

At the battle of Kurukshetra Bhishma commanded the army of the Kauravas and during the first nine days he slew 90,000 warriors. The Pandavas felt that he was taking more than his share and Arjuna was selected to kill him. Now Bhishma had in his youth vowed that he would never raise his hand against either a woman or a eunuch. So Arjuna at Krishna's advice advanced against Bhishma behind the eunuch Shikhundi. Bhishma seeing only the eunuch declined to retaliate. Thus Arjuna shot him several times before he discovered the trick. Then when he advanced in turn on Arjuna, Yudhishtira called all his soldiers to his brother's help. They drove back the Kauravas and forming a circle round Bhishma fired volleys of arrows into him until not two fingers' space in his body remained unwounded. At last he fell from his chariot and the gods and the demons alike sorrowed at his fall. Here I will translate from Messrs. Chiplunkar and Co.'s Marathi version.

"When long armed Bhishma King of Archers fell with the shock of Indra's thunderbolt, then all earth shivered. But as his body was covered entirely with arrows none of it touched the ground and he remained supported above it by the Pandava's darts. . . . But just before Bhishma had fallen fainting from his chariot, he had seen that the sun was to the south and that it was the Dakshinayan. And therefore, O Bharata, he would not close his eyes, but knowing that the time was inauspicious he returned to consciousness. Moreover in the heavens a celestial voice was heard saying 'O Tiger among men, O son of Ganges skilled in arms, O great one, will you die now that it is Dakshinayan.' Hearing the voice, the son of Ganga answered 'I am holding my life back; I shall not let it escape.' And as he lay on the ground that Prince of the Kurus held back his life and waited for the sun to turn northward. And Ganga, daughter of Himalaya, knowing his resolve sent to Bhishma, Rishis in the guise of Swans. And the Swans fled from the Manas* lake to where Bhishma

* This lake has recently been discovered and described by Dr. Swen Hedin. The circling (Pradakshina) was to do Bhishma honour.

lay on his bed of arrows. And when they saw the Kuru chief they circled round him and beheld the sun to the southward. Then they spoke one to the other and said 'what would be said if Bhishma for all his strength were to die in the Dakshinayan.' So saying they flew away to the southward. But Bhishma wise above all men thought for a moment and said 'O Swans, verily I tell you that come what may, as long as the sun lingers in the south so long I shall not depart heavenwards.' When Aditya* shall go northwards then only will I go thither whence I came. Therefore I shall hold fast my life and shall stay here longing for the solstice. Nor shall I fail. For to let my life go when I like is within my power. For the boon that my father Shantanu, the mighty, gave me was this 'Thou shalt have the gift of dying when it listeth thee.' Thus, O Swans, let me enjoy this gift of mine. And if the power of letting my life go free, is in my hands, then I shall surely hold it fast till the sun turns northwards."

The Kshattriya chief was as good as his word. The warriors of both armies dug round him a ditch to keep away the wild beasts. And he lingered on his bed of arrows until the 8th Magh Sudha, when the sun turned northward. Then he let his spirit go free. Heaven's gates were flung wide. And the Kuru warrior was received with acclamation.

---

* The sun.

III.

THE LION'S FORTRESS.

A BALLAD OF SINHGAD.

THE following ballad is an adaptation rather than a translation of the Marathi ballad in Acworth and Saligram's collection which celebrates the capture of Sinhgad, or the Lion's fort, a well-known stronghold 13 miles from Poona. In July, 1665, Shivaji had been forced by the Moghuls to sue for peace and sign the treaty of Purandhar. By its terms Shivaji surrendered 20 forts and became an officer of the Moghul Emperor. Shivaji fulfilled his part of the treaty faithfully enough. But after he had been invited to Delhi and there detained, he considered that he was no longer bound by it. This view his mother Jijibai cordially supported. And the ballad describes how, roused by the sight of Sinhgad in the distance, she sent for her son and challenged him to a game of dice. She prayed for help to Bhawani, the goddess of Pratapgad, and by her assistance she won. As a forfeit Jijibai claimed Sinhgad. Shivaji protested. The garrison was strong. Udai Bhan, the Rathor Commandant, was a famous swordsman. His strength and prowess were such that he had no less than eighteen wives. He had 12 sons as brave as himself and a man-slaying elephant called Chandravelly. But Jijibai would take no refusal. Shivaji at last thought of Tanaji Malusre, the Subhedar of Umrathe, in the Konkan, and sent him the "Vida" or rolled betel leaf, which was a sign that Shivaji wanted his assistance for a forlorn hope. Tanaji took the "Vida," and scaled the fort by means of a rope attached to Shivaji's ghorpad Yeshwant. On Tanaji's reaching its summit with 50 men, the rope broke. Nevertheless he killed Chandravelly and Udai, Bhan's 12 sons, but was himself killed by Udai Bhan. Then the remaining Marathas, making their way through one of the gates forced open by the supernatural aid of Bhawani, overpowered and slaughtered the garrison and their Commandant. The date of the escalade was 9th February 1670.

'Twas Queen Jijibai looked forth to the East and to the North,
As at Pratapgad one morning she combed her raven hair.
And white as ivory seeming, with the sunlight on it streaming,
The Lion's fort was gleaming in the February air.
"Now my messenger come hither; go ride to Rajgad, thither
"Tell Shivaji of Junnar that his mother needs him sore!"
And the messenger rode far by Madha and by Par
And he thundered through Birwadi and he flashed through Poladpore.
Now to Rajgad he has ridden and to enter he is bidden.
"Why comest thou thus unsummoned and why comest thou in such haste?"
"Tis Queen Jijibai has cried, till my son is at my side
"No water shall I drink and no morsel shall I taste."
"Bring my shield and breast-plate here, bring my tiger claws and spear.
"Lead Krishna from the stables, the pride of all the stud!

"For by Madha and by Par, by the Moon and by the star
"Shivaji of Junnar must ride to Pratapgad."
The blare of his horn woke Queen Jijibai at morn.
"Come Shivaji of Junnar, I would play at dice with thee."
And the wager was taken and the dice box was shaken.
"Bhavani," prayed Queen Jijibai, "grant victory to me."
From her shrine above the valley high o'er Par and Ambenali,
Bhavani heard and ordered it that Shivaji should lose.
And thrown by either hand the dice at her command
For Jijibai shewed sixes and for Shivaji fell twos.
"Now choose, mother mine, from my strongholds twenty-nine
"Choose Rajgad or Raigad or Gheri by the sea,
"Choose Makrangad or Chandan, choose Visapur or Wandan."
"Nay Shivaji of Junnar, give the Lion's fort to me."
Then the Bhosle's brow grew black, as he slowly muttered back:
"But Udai Bhan, the Rathor, and his 12 sons guard the way
"He has Arabs and Afghans and Rajputs and Pathans."
"Nay the Lion's fortress give me ; 'twas a wager ; thou must pay."
"But the elephant Chandravelly, the man-slayer from Delhi,
Will trample us to powder, if we break their fighting line."
"Now God's curse upon thee rest, if thou dost not my behest.
"But on thee a mother's blessing when the Lion's fort is mine."
Both back to Rajgad went, but a weary night he spent.
"Now who among my barons all will win the hold for me ?

"To win it went forth many but there came back never any;
"Oft planted was the mango seed, but nowhere grows the tree.
"Where the emerald Konkan rests 'neath the Sahyadri's crests
"Dwells Tanaji the Lion, my boldest baron he.
"Now my messenger ride back down the rugged Madha track
"And with 12,000 men at arms call Tanaji to me."
Swift the horseman crossed the Doni on his nimble Deccan pony—
The little Doni water that lives but through the rains—
Then a-down the sunny slopes to the verdant mango topes,
That nestled round Umrathe in the pleasant Konkan plains.
Through the outer gate he rode, through the Darbar hall he strode,
Where Tanaji Malusre has seated him in state:
"'Tis the Bhosle who has spoken. See! I bring his betel token
"And he calls thee with thy vassals and he bids thee not be late."
"Ho! gather Wadghar Naiks from your rice fields and your dykes,
"Ho! Shirkes of Umrathe your sturdy tenants bring,
"Ho! fly o'er Nandiv manor the Savant's knightly banner
"And speed ye with your liege lord Malusre to the King."
With sword on shoulder hung, on his steed Malusre sprung,
When his son the dark-eyed Rayaba his father craved to see.
"My father, prithee tarry, for to-morrow morn I marry
"With the fairest in the Konkan with the bride hast picked for me."

" When Ganga backward flows at the melting of the snows
" When Yamuna rolls her waters from Prayag to Khatmandhu,
" Then only then by Hari ! shall I tarry, shalt thou marry,
" When Shivaji of Junnar has work for me to do."
They have reached Rajgad and wait. " Fling wide the Hirva gate
" Oh Shivaji of Junnar, was thy token but a jest ?"
" Nay Queen Jijibai did need thee, her lips alone shall speed thee ;
" My mother, tell thy champion his guerdon and his quest."
She waved around his head her five-wicked lamp and said :
" Of all the Bhosle's barons men shall deem thee as the first.
" Nay, I shall be thy mother and Shivaji thy brother
" If thou wrest the Lion's fortress from the rule of the accurst."
To her feet he bowed his crest : " Be thy heart, O Queen, at rest,
" He who bears a mother's blessing is safe from every !
" And be thou at my side my hand and blade to guide
" O Bhavani of Pratapgad, Bhavani of the hill !"
They have reached the broken ground, the Lion's fort around,
And they've freed the ghorpad Yeshwant beneath the western gate
They have flung a necklace o'er him and bent the knee before him
And they've tied the rope around him that should bear them to their fate.
Half way the ghorpad turned for the soul within him learned
That the fortress frowning o'er him soon would see Malusre die
And the armed men behind him cried : " O Tanaji, unbind him
" Defeat and death await us for the ghorpad cannot lie."

Loud laughed Malusre scorning the ghorpad Yeshwant's warning,
"And if Hell yawned before us should a Kshattriya hesitate?
"If that lazy beast plays prophet, I shall soon make mince-meat of it
"And I'll cook it on chapattis and we'll eat it while we wait."
Then the frightened ghorpad fled up the dark rock overhead
Till above he fixed his talons deeply, firmly in the heath.
And their hearts beat high with hope as they scaled the swinging rope
With their blankets round their faces and their tulwars in their teeth.
Fifty men, a chosen band, on the bastion's summit stand,
When the rope breaks behind them as ye snap a strand at will.
"Now Kshattriyas stand fast! For the cause! For the caste!
"For Shivaji of Junnar and Bhavani of the Hill!"
On hands and knees they crept where the Arab guardsmen slept
Of the sleep that comes unbroken from the wine when it is red.
Then a silent sudden dart and a knife thrust to the heart
And they slew the whole 900 save a single one who fled.
He fled on wings of fear to the castle's top-most tier
Where Udai Bhan was toying with his 18 ladies fair.
"Lo! the Kafir from the west he has slaughtered all thy best
"Leave thy revels and thy ladies or we lose the Lion's lair."
Then Udai Bhan looked up as he quaffed his golden cup
"Now a curse upon the Kafir and a plague upon thy head.
"Send the elephant Chandravelly, the man-slayer from Delhi.
"He will trample down the Kafir like the worm beneath his tread."

They have drugged the brute with bhang till his trunk in fury swung
And his eye-balls glared as red as the Sun at even-tide.
"Now yield thou country lout," cried in scorn the bold Mahout,
"Or be trampled into powder under Chandravelly's stride."
Fierce waxed Malusre's ire and his Konkan blood took fire.
And he sprang astride the monster and his kick the driver slew.
Then his tulwar downward sped, where the trunk met tusks and head
And the man-slayer sank lifeless as the singing blade shore through.
"Udai Bhan be up and doing or all Islam will be rueing.
"Chandravelly," cried the Arab, "lies a lump of bleeding clay."
"Send my 12 sons to the battle, they will drive the foe like cattle
"But my 18 winsome ladies I shall love them while I may."
Stamped on each bold stripling's face was his regal Rajput race—
All the fiery soul of Marwad flashing bright through every eye—
Like the crag a-down the correi, like the tiger on the quarry,
They rushed upon Malusre to kill him or to die.
Swift aside Malusre stept and as each one forward leapt,
He smote him through the shoulder all a-down the sacred string
And they died without a sigh for the cruel Chagatai*
With their faces towards the foeman and their backs upon the ling.
Then the Arab told their doom in the merry bridal room,
Where the Rathor loved the ladies who sighed for him alone.

---

* Chagatai or Jagatai was the tribal name of that branch of the Mongols from whom the Moghul emperors were descended.

"Now thy gallant sons are slain, durst thou Delhi face again
"And the laughter of the nobles and the anger of the throne?"
Lo! Udai Bhan has sprung where his sword and buckler hung;
In a single line he's placed them, his 18 ladies fair.
And his blade flashed through and through them as one and all he slew them
And lightly touched their life-blood on his forehead and his hair.
Now Bhavani of the Hill guard brave Tanaji from ill,
For the stoutest hand might tremble and the boldest heart might fear
For in duel or in melee the deftest blade in Delhi
Was this mighty Rajput captain of the Moghul Alamgir.
As the lightning flash descends where the Indryani wends,
When the thunder clouds are gathered round Visapur in Jesht.
On Malusre fell the blow beating sword and sword-arm low
And Tanaji the Lion fell cloven to the waist.
Bhavani from her fane sorrowed sorely o'er the slain
"Deep and dark shall be the vengeance ere his soul to Kailas go."
And the breath of her hate burst wide the Kalyan-gate
And Tanaji's 12,000 sprang headlong on the foe.
Then the good Maratha steel clove the Rathor to the heel
And the rest they dragged in triumph to the Kalyan-gate to kill.
And the blood of the accurst* ran free to quench the thirst
Of Bhavani of Pratapgad, Bhavani of the Hill.

---

* I trust my Musulman readers will not take offence at the word 'accurst.' It is the nearest translation in English of the word Mleccha, which Hindus bestow on all of other religions than their own. And it was the phrase which the English Puritans bestowed on their High-church countrymen.

On a cot their chief they laid, by his side his blood-stained blade,
And the conquered guns roared homage as they bore him down the *Khind.*
And no throne could have been fitter than that rude triumphal litter
For a baron of the Konkan for a Kshattriya of Ind.
And they bore him back again to the sunny Konkan plain.
To his old fief of Umrathe where his fathers lived and died.
Twelve days the King wept o'er him for the great love that he bore him
And the next he chose for Rayaba, a fairer, luckier bride.
Then he sent a workman skilled a monument to build
On the Lion's fortress' summit on the spot where he was slain.
For all Maharashtra through, where the Bhagva Jhenda blew,
His like ne'er lived before him and shall never live again.
And there carved in stone *virasan* *, still he looks o'er lake and station,
Ringed round with desolation, where the grey apes leap and swing.
And clear as history's pages he tells the after ages
How Tanaji the Lion won the Fortress for the King.†

---

* Virasan is the attitude of the warrior when seated.

† This ballad has been published as an appendix to Prof. Rawlinson's "Shivaji."

IV.

AN INDIAN HAMLET.

IT is not often that a writer sits down to write a play with the avowed intention of imitating Shakespeare. It is still less often that having done so, a writer proposes to embody in it both Hamlet and Iago. And Mr. Khadilkar is probably the only instance of such a writer having attained success. In a very interesting preface Mr. Khadilkar has explained that while studying English at College, he formed the idea of writing a Marathi play which combined the hero of Hamlet and the villain of Othello; and that while reading Mr. Khare's life of Nana Phadnavis, it occurred to him that the Peshwa Madhavrao II* resembled in many respects the Prince of Denmark. Mr. Khadilkar's next step was to search for a suitable Iago. As there was no historical parallel he had recourse to his imagination and he invented a villain similar to the famous Italian out of a Brahman beggar in the service of the pretender Bajirao Raghunathrao. There is no mention in history of any such person. But as scandalous stories about Nana Phadnavis were sedulously spread by the pretender's adherents and seem to have

* Savai Madhavrao yancha mrityu by Mr. K. P. Khadilkar (Chitrashala Press), Madhavrao II is always known in Maratha history as Savai or 1¼ Madhavrao. It is said that when he was a child it was prophesied of him that he would 1¼ times as great as his distinguished uncle.

reached the ears of Madhavrao II, Mr. Khadilkar thought himself justified in concluding that they did so through just such a person. A story is related of Flaubert that he once wrote what he thought was a masterpiece, and on its completion called a few favoured friends to hear him read it. When he had reached the end he waited complacently for their reverential applause. One and all, however, exclaimed "Burn it!" He took their advice, chose a fresh subject, formed a fresh style and wrote the incomparable Madame Bovary. A somewhat similar experience befell Mr. Khadilkar. After his play had appeared in a Marathi magazine one of his friends criticized it so severely that Mr. Khadilkar almost entirely rewrote it. Even then he was not permitted to escape scot free. For one ill-conditioned critic wrote that it would have been best if Mr. Khadilkar had never been born, but as this could not now be helped the next best thing was for him to die quickly!

This is certainly a most unfair criticism. And the genuine merit of Mr. Khadilkar's play has been proved on the stage wherein the later version has been warmly welcomed. And I have hopes that its literary excellence and the sources of its inspiration may make it interesting to English readers. Fully, however, to understand it one must, for a moment, revive one's acquaintance with Deccan history. In the year 1772 there died of consumption at Theur Madhavrao the first, one of the most capable princes who ever adorned a throne. At the age of 16 called to supreme place at a time of supreme disaster, he laboured unceasingly and successfully to restore the good estate of Poona. And when he died at the age of 28, he left the Chitpavan empire once more great and prosperous. He was succeeded by his younger brother Narayanrao, conspicuous among whose ministers, was one Balaji Janardhan Bhanu now usually described as Nana* Phadnavis. The family of this eminent Indian statesman had long been connected with the rulers of Poona. Before either the Bhanus or the Bhats had climbed the Western ghats, their families resided, the former at Vel and the latter at Shiwardhan, not far from the fort of Janjira. The heads of the families were respectively Balaji and Janoji Bhat and Balaji Mahdev Bhanu. For some unknown cause the Sidi of Janjira seized Janoji Bhat and tying him in a sack flung him into the sea. His brother escaped and fled with his friend Bhanu to King Shahu's Court at Satara. There both found employment and his extraordinary shrewdness and industry raised Balaji Bhat to the post of Peshwa. For several generations the family connection continued and in 1763 Nana Balaji Janardhan Bhanu was in his cousin Moraba's place raised to the post of Phadnavis or controller of the treasury. For several years he held this high office, but he did not attain to real power until death had removed the able Prince who tolerated in his dominions no rival to himself. Madhavrao I's younger brother and successor Narayanrao was of a less stern mould and Nana Phadnavis soon acquired a preponderating influence. On the 30th August 1773, Narayanrao was murdered at his aunt Anandibai's instigation and with his uncle Raghunathrao's connivance and the latter hoped to reap the

* Nana is a common diminutive of Balaji. Balaji Bajirao, the 3rd Peshwa, was usually spoken of as the Nana Sahib.

benefits of the crime. But Nana's high-minded refusal to remain in office under him and the posthumous birth of Narayanrao's son Madhavrao defeated the uncle's hopes and during twenty years secured for Nana as regent for the minor the undisputed sovereignty of the Deccan. They were not, however, years free from trouble and difficulty and under less able guidance the ship of state might well have foundered. Raghunathrao, until his death, struggled with tireless energy to usurp the Poona throne. And his claims obtained in turn support from the English, the Nizam and Sultan Tipu of Maisur. But in 1795, Nana Phadnavis had reached the summit of human glory. His reputation as financier, statesman and even as general was unrivalled. The English attempt to enthrone Ragthunathrao had ended in disaster. The Nizam's pride had been humbled at Kharda. Tipu had twice been forced to sue for peace. And for the last time in Deccan history the great jaghirdars worked submissively for the crown. There was, however, one dark cloud on the horizon. Raghunathrao's children had survived him and were state prisoners at Shivner. The eldest Bajirao was nineteen, thus only one year younger than the ruling prince. Bajirao's personal attractions, too, were far above the common. Alike in horsemanship and archery, in scholarship and in charm he had no equal in Western India. But Nana guessed rightly that the fair exterior concealed a scheming and treacherous heart. He had inherited his mother's wickedness and his father's ambition and his sole desire was to win his consin's confidence and then rob him of his throne. The regent warned Madhavrao but in vain and a secret correspondence began between the cousins. It was discovered by Nana, and to prevent its repetition Madhavrao was confined in the Shanwarvada and the rigour of Bajirao's imprisonment was increased. Not long afterwards, Madhavrao who deeply felt this treatment either fell or threw himself—the question is not free from doubt—from the palace balcony and after a series of desperate intrigues, his cousin Bajirao succeeded him on the throne. The death of Madhavrao ruined Nana Phadnavis and indirectly the dominion of the Peshwas. It is in the closing scenes of this reign that Mr. Khadilkar has laid the scenes of his play. And the theme of it is that Madhavrao's death was really brought about by the machinations of his cousin. When the curtain rises, the spectator is informed that the prince's father-in-law Baba Sahib has been banished and that Bajirao's warder Nagnath has been condemned to death for having been privy to the cousin's secret correspondence. Nothing daunted, Bajirao has plunged into a deeper plot. One Keshav Shastri, his confidential agent, has, in the disguise of a mendicant Brahman and astrologer, obtained admittance to Madhavrao's Court. Openly he affects to condemn the imprisoned pretender. Secretly he strives with diabolical ingenuity to make a breach between the Peshwa and the regent. He at first pretends to have a message to deliver from the banished Baba Sahib to his daughter Madhavrao's queen. The prince's curiosity is aroused and asks that he should be told what it is. Keshav Shastri begs to be excused, prays that he may be forgiven, but at last, when positively ordered to do so, blurts it out with great emphasis. It was to the effect that he (Baba Sahib) was not going to be Nana's creature* like the Peshwa. Any one who desired the throne had of course to fawn on Nana. Like a bullock with a ring through its nose he had to turn and twist as Nana made him. But as for himself (Baba Sahib) he wanted neither a place in the household or elsewhere. He had a small country estate and he would just go and live there in independence. No words could be better calculated to increase the Peshwa's growing jealousy of the all-powerful regent and as the first scene closes, Keshavshastri chuckles aside that his first device, or mantra as he styles it, has succeeded and Madhavrao, left alone on the stage, pours out a tirade against his own servitude. He is afraid, he admits, in the presence of Nana, yet he recalls that his ancestors, Bajirao I and Balaji II and his uncle Madhavrao, at an even earlier age than his, led armies to victory. He resolves to assert himself and an opportunity for doing so soon arrives. The English Ambassador Malet has requested the Poona Government to allow the Company to trade within the Peshwa's territories. Nana Phadnavis, who has no liking for the English, wishes peremptorily to refuse. Madhavrao, who has been fascinated by Malet's charm and is anxious to thwart the regent, disagrees and declares that he will reserve the matter for his own consideration. Nana Phadnavis is naturally nettled and when immediately afterwards Nagnath's punishment has to be finally considered, insists on confirming the death sentence. Madhavrao, although anxious to

* The Marathi is tatakhalche manzar, *i.e.*, the cat waiting beneath the plate for food. The closest translation would be 'tame cat' had that not acquired a peculiar meaning of its own.

save a man in whose only crime he is himself implicated, is frightened again to interfere. Nagnath is taken away to die. But before he leaves the stage he turns furiously on the faithless prince and tells him that he is no true Peshwa but the child of Nana. Nagnath's meaning is purely figurative but his saying will soon have terrible results. As I have already mentioned Baba Sahib, the Peshwa's father-in-law, has been banished for his connivance at the correspondence of the cousins. The Peshwa's wife Yeshoda, who is still a child, is very angry at her father's punishment. And the regent hoping .to appease her gives Baba Sahib's place in the household to Yeshoda's mother known as the Ai Sahib or, to use a famous historical parallel, Madame Mère. Yeshoda is fully satisfied, but Keshavshastri does not fail to turn to his own account this appointment just as he has done Baba Sahib's banishment. In the course of the first act he suggests to Madhavrao that Madame Mère and Nana Phadnavis seem always to be talking together and then gradually insinuates that Baba Sahib used to complain of their improper intimacy. Next he observes that he has just received a letter from him. The Peshwa asks to see it. Keshavshastri again affects to object. And when at last ordered to do so under pain of death, he gives the prince a forged note in which Baba Sahib writes positively that there is an intrigue between his wife and the regent, that he himself has been banished to facilitate it and that he suspects Yeshoda of being Nana's child. The unfortunate young prince, who remembers that it was Nana who arranged his marriage, readily believes the story and the curtain falls as he denounces in burning words the wickedness of the minister. At the beginning of the third act the audience is told that the Peshwa is ill. In reality his mind has been deeply affected by the lying story of Keshavshastri and at the ensuing Durbar he is unable to treat the regent with even ordinary civility. The Peshwa's tormentor, however, soon finds an opportunity of aggravating his malady. The British Ambassador has sent to the Court three portraits drawn by the English artist, Mr. Wales, of Madhavrao himself, of his queen Yeshoda and of Nana Phadnavis. In a scene written with consummate skill, Keshavshastri makes the young prince believe that he and his wife Yeshoda both resemble the regent. This leads Madhavrao to the horrible inference that Nana had formerly an intrigue with his (Madhavrao's) deceased mother and that he and Yeshoda are really brother and sister. I translate the following portion :

Keshavshastri : "If Your Highness will look, you will see how exactly Nana's features are depicted (*i.e.*, in Wales' portrait). With what skill the man's nature is revealed in the painting!"

Madhavrao*: "Is all Nana's baseness revealed in it?"

Keshavshastri : "The artist has drawn three portraits. First look at Nana's. See that long neck, those piercing eyes, that long proud face, how they show love of authority, over-bearing pride and exceptional intelligence. Such, indeed, is his ambition to be above everybody, such is his wish to be taller than the rest that his

---

* Madhavrao, I take it means that he has a long face also and will, therefore, be able to hold his own. The remark, however, gives Keshavshastri an opportunity of insinuating that he is really like Nana in appearance.

face has lengthened itself so as to add height to his body. Just such was the face of Haidar who robbed his master of his kingdom."

Madhavrao: "But I have a long face too?"

Keshavshastri: "But see; how terrible to all is Nana's slanting look, what vile vices lay in wait for him who turns his back on the straight road of virtue. Every footstep is crooked, every act is crooked!"

Madhavrao: "You do not think my glance is slanting, do you?"

Keshavshastri: "There must, of course, be some reserve and some adroitness in those called to the throne. It is, therefore, true that there is some resemblance between Nana's face and Your Highness. But in Your Highness's face virtues stand in the place of Nana's vices. A quality becomes a vice or a virtue according to circumstances. Indeed there must be some resemblance between your two faces. Is there anything strange if the creator, when He in His infinite wisdom created two men, one to be king and one to be minister, should have, in order to show the tie between them, bound them together by the bond of physical resemblance?"

Madhavrao: "But how could this likeness show itself in our faces?"

Keshavshastri: "Will your Highness just look at Her Highness's picture? You see her neck is rather long. Her face is rather drawn."

Madhavrao: "Yes that is so."

Keshavshastri: "Your Highness, those who are united by ties of love, those whose life must be passed, almost in one manner, whose good and evil deeds, whose happiness and grief are for ever joined, may well have some outward similarity, may they not ?"

Madhavrao: "I can quite understand that hers and Nana's faces should be like each other. But my face—O! what do you say? What do you mean?"

Keshavshastri seeing that the horrible suspicion has taken root in the young man's mind gives an evasive answer and begs him to listen to a ballad-singer whom he has introduced into the palace for the purpose of cheering His Highness. In reality the ballad-singer is another agent of Bajirao. He sings two ballads. The first is of an ordinary pattern and is in praise of Nana's bravery at Kharda. It is merely intended further to irritate the prince against the regent. But the next is alleged to have been composed by (Bajirao) himself. Madhavrao's interest is at once aroused and he listens to it intently. To his horror it converts his fearful suspicion of his own and Yeshoda's parentage into a certainty. In it the Peshwa is described as being Bhanu's offspring in the same words that Nagnath used. These now flash into the mind of the unhappy boy and he runs on the verge of madness to his room. Having reached this point Mr. Khadilkar should have hastened as quickly as possible to the climax of the play. But, no doubt, influenced by his desire to make the young Chitpavan resemble Hamlet, he has delayed the progress of the tale by introducing several scenes between the former and his wife modelled on those between the Dane and Ophelia. In reality the remainder of the story is very simple. Obsessed by the horrible idea that his mother and his mother-in-law have alike been the mistresses of Nana and that his wife is also his sister, his madness becomes worse and worse. During the Dasara ceremonies he tries to commit suicide by throwing himself off his elephant. For this he is kept in close restraint in the Shanwarwada palace, but ultimately he eludes his guardians and leaping from the balcony of the 3rd story, falls into the court-yard, and is killed. When the fatal event happens the minister is announcing to his council that he has unearthed Keshavshastri's villany. The latter's forged letters have been discovered ; the jewels paid him as the price of his daring have been found on him ; and his mistress who was fully in his confidence has made a clean breast of her lover's wickedness. The latter's sentence has just been determined when a scared attendant enters in with the terrible news. And the curtain drops as Nana Phadnavis exclaims the tragic and prophetic words : "With His Highness' fall, the Maratha empire has crashed to pieces !"

In estimating the merits of the play it is impossible not to feel the frankest admiration for the character of the regent, as Mr. Khadilkar has drawn him. The great statesman looking back on 20 years of extraordinary difficulties met and conquered, on victories won in turn against three rival powers at Wadgaon and Panvel Kharde and Badami can boast and with reason that in no long time he will fulfil the dying wish of Madhavrao the Great, that soon the Afghans will be driven beyond the North-West passes and that once more the yellow flag will dance above the fort of Attack. Yet in spite of his great achievements he never lacks deference to his young master. Repeatedly thwarted and insulted by the unreasonable boy, Nana Phadnavis never loses his self-control. And if towards the end of the play he feels bound to confine him in the Shanwarwada, it is clear alike both to council and audience that his sole aim is the young prince's good. Nor can the highest praise be denied to Keshavshastri, Mr. Khadilkar's Indian Iago. Even the Italian himself is hardly more fiendishly plausible, more diabolically subtle. But the play would undoubtedly have been of even greater excellence than it is, had the author not tried to mould his hero on the tragic figure of Elsinore. Indeed to combine Iago and Hamlet in a single play is a superhuman task. All the other characters in the play must be completely subordinated if the strange moody nature of the Dane is fully to be appreciated. Again there is hardly any real resemblance between Mr. Khadilkar's and Shakespeare's heroes. Hamlet had been by his uncle cheated of his birth-right. Madhavrao occupied the throne solely owing to the regent's rectitude and ability. Hamlet* was 30 years old. Madhavrao is barely 20. And lastly Madhavrao goes mad while Hamlet only pretended to. Why the latter feigned insanity puzzled Johnson and appears to have misled Mr. Khadilkar. His conduct, however, seems really to have been consistent throughout. He was, to use his own words, "a dull and muddy mettled rascal." He was as fat and scant of breath in soul as in body, and although when worked up to fever heat, he could strike at Polonius and kill the king, yet in ordinary affairs he snatched at any pretext which enabled him to postpone action. He lost his best chance of killing his uncle while at prayer, for the ridiculous

* Hamlet's age is to be found in Act v., Scene 1.

reason that he did not wish, "to take him in the purging of his soul." This was a mere excuse for inactivity. In the same way he seeems to have feigned madness so as to cheat himself into the belief that he was taking vigorous steps when he was really doing nothing. As a matter of fact a character whom Mr. Khadilkar's prince resembles far more than he does Hamlet is the Duc de Reichstadt in M. Rostand's Aiglon. The two youths were about the same age. They were both overawed by all-powerful ministers—the one by Bhanu, the other by Metternich. Both were mere dreamers 'jeunes Byroniens' to use the Duc de Reichstadt's phrase. Both were spurred to action by memories of mighty names. In both cases their struggle to free themselves were quieted for ever by untimely deaths. And, indeed, Mr. Khadilkar could hardly have closed his work and answered his critics more appropriately than by the fine lines of M. Rostand's epilogue :

"Et maintenant il faut que ton altesse dorme,
Ame pour qui la Mort est une guérison—
Dorme, au fond du caveau, dans la double prison
De son cercucil de bronze et de cet uniforme
Qu'un vain paperassier cherche, gratte et s'informe
Même quand il a tort, le poète a raison

* * * * *

Dors, ce n'est pas toujours la légende qui ment
Un reve est moins trompeur, parfois, qu'un document.
Dors ; tu fus ce Jeune homme et ce fils, quoi qu'on dise."

V.

AN UNTOUCHABLE SAINT.

CHOKHAMELA.

PANDHARPUR on the banks of the Bhima river is not a place often visited by English visitors. And the few officials who do halt there are, as a rule, too busy to examine it with much care. Yet the spot is well worth a careful visit. It is the chief place in India, where Vishnu is worshipped in his avatar of Vithoba or Vithal. And it was the seat of a mighty movement which helped, more than perhaps any other cause, to compass the emancipation of Maharashtra.

Although, probably, a very ancient shrine, it did not become famous until the beginning of the 13th century. This century was, in many respects, the most momentous in the history of Southern India. In 1192 A. D., Mahomed Ghori had at Narain defeated Rai Pithora and had founded the Musulman empire of Delhi. The arms of Islam did not at once penetrate south of the Vindhyas. But the close proximity of a strange and foreign rule had on the Yadav Government at Devgiri, much the same effect, that the establishment of the Spaniards in the Carbbean Sea had on the Aztecs of Mexico. Everywhere a ferment began to manifest itself. Strange prophecies became current. Heretical doctrines denying the efficacy of caste began everywhere to circulate. And when, early in the 13th century, Dnyandev, outcasted at Alandi, boldly pronounced at Pandharpur that faith was better than sacrifices and attacked Brahman supremacy by translating into Marathi the Bhagwadgita, he soon founded a numerous and powerful sect. Finally, the Devgiri Kingdom, bewildered by the mental ferment that affected its subjects, fell in 1294 before the assault of only 700 soldiers. Under the Musulman rulers who succeeded the Yadavs, the Pandharpur sect obtained increasing influence and produced saints and poets in ever-growing numbers. But it accomplished its supreme achievement when, at the beginning of the 14th century, a Mhar worshipper at Vithoba's shrine attained, during his life, canonisation and was, after his death, declared by many to have been an incarnation of Vishnu.

The name of this remarkable personage was Chokha mela. And the legend preserved by the Mhar community is as follows. His father and mother Sudama and Muktabai lived at Anagod near Pandharpur. Although they owned no less than half the village vatan lands, they were childless and unhappy. In order to obtain offspring, Sudama made 244 pilgrimages to Pandharpur. One day in his absence, it fell to Muktabai to convey 200 mangoes from the Mhar lands to be divided by the Musulman Governor of Bedar. As she walked, a starving Brahman met her and asked her for some mangoes. She, at first, refused because, until the Musulman Governor had allotted them, she was forbidden to dispose of them. But the Brahman fell on the ground and threatened to die unless he was fed. So Muktabai yielded and gave him 5 mangoes. The hungry man ate them all and then gave her his blessing. "You gave me 5 mangoes," he said, "you shall, therefore, have 5 children. Call the eldest Chokha because I have sucked (chokhnen) the mangoes." With these words he vanished. When Muktabai reached Bedar, the Governor's clerk reported that she was very late and that instead of 200 she had brought 205 mangoes. The Governor asked her explanation. She told her story. And the Governor who, although of another faith, was yet a pious man, let her go in peace. For he believed her and guessed that she had fed a god and that he had repaid her gift twofold.

In due course a son was born to Muktabai, and received the name of Chokha or Chokhamela. Trained by pious parents, he grew up a saintly boy. And the legend has it that his saintliness brought him a rich reward. As a Mhar, it was his duty to drag the bodies of dead cattle from the vicinity of the villagers' houses. One day he happened to be the only Mhar present in Anagod, and he was ordered to drag away the body of a large cow that had just died. The task was too great for the half grown lad. But Vishnu came to his help and with this divine assistance the task was easily performed. When it was finished, a high born maiden, who had been permitted to see the god, threw herself at Chokhamela's feet and implored him to accept her as his bride. So signal a proof of divine favour led Chokhamela to abandon his home in Anagod and to take up his residence at Pandharpur. As a Mhar he could not enter the temples. But he prayed continuously to Vishnu from the outer gate. The thought, however, of a Mhar saint was too much even for the followers of Dnyandev and the persecution, which befell him there and his eventual triumph, form the subject of a graceful poem by Mahipati. In all humility I have translated it into English couplets, which give the sense, although not the charm of the original.

One day, as Chokhamela from afar
Worshipped at Pandhari Vishnu's avatar,
A Brahman scoffed at him and said " I pray,
" Tell me what good are all the prayers you say.
" You worship Vishnu both by day and night,
" Yet may not venture in his holy sight.
" Your prayers to Him are as a dog should wish
" To eat with Brahmans from a Brahman dish.
" A beggarman shall win a Royal mate.
" Long ere you enter inside Vishnu's gate ;
" The wandering waif, as through the woods he gropes,
" *May* reach the Wishing tree and crown his hopes ;
" The dying man *may* find the Amrit[1] jar,
" But Vishnu *never* looks upon a Mhar."
Then Chokhamela glanced at him and sighed
And, humbly bowing to the earth, replied :
" The sun, though parted by unnumbered miles,
" Still on the lotus sheds his radiant smiles ;
" The moon, though high and higher still she soar,
" Spurns not the passion of the fond chikor.
" So, too, High heaven's lord may yet incline
" Hope of the helpless, to this prayer of mine.
" From far the mother runs her young to save,
" From far He sees and shrinks not from the slave.
" But if He finds no temple in your heart,
" Close to His shrine, you yet are far apart."

[1] Amrit is the drink which gives immortality.

That night the Discus Bearer came and stood
By the saint's cot of worn and broken wood.
Then bore him swiftly to His temple hall
And placed him in the holiest spot of all.
In His the saint's hand taking, He confessed
His was the worship which had pleased Him best.
A temple priest, who slept outside, awoke
And calling to the other priests thus spoke :
"See ! Chokhamela or some other Mhar
"Sits by the shrine with Vishnu's avatar,
"Through the locked doors the outcaste tracked his prey,
"The cloud-dark God robed, jewelled as the Day.
"As when the queen of night in fullest grace
"Is wrapped by Rahu [1] in his foul embrace.
"Or when grim Ketu [1] seizes and devours
"The Sun when shining through the noon-day hours,
"So sprang the Mhar and swift pollution spread
"O'er Vaikunth's [2] Lord as He the Vedas read.
"God is defiled ! and O ! thrice cursed deed !
"Fled is the faith and fouled the Brahmans' creed."
They seized the saint and dragged him through the door.
"Now get ye hence beyond the Bhima's shore !"
The saint implored their pardon all in vain.
"Begone" they answered "lest ye sin again ;
"Hell is his portion, who hath God defiled."
But Chokhamela said and softly smiled :
"Nay if a Mhar should bathe in Ganga's tide,
"Will his pollution in Her stream abide ?
"Or, when the southern wind sweeps o'er the plain,
"Is it infected by the outcaste's stain ?
"The sun's reflection in a pool may lie ;
"But yet the sun itself leaves not the sky.

---

[1] Lunar eclipses are believed to be caused by Rahu swallowing the Moon, and solar eclipses by Ketu swallowing the Sun.

[2] Vaikuntha is Vishnu's heaven.

" Base though I be, no evil have I done
" Him in whose eyes all castes and creeds are one.
" Indeed your speech but ill befits the wise."
To him the temple priest with blazing eyes :
" And shall the Mhar unto the twice born teach
" The lore religious in his low born speech ?
" Shall Vishnu's Garud [1] from the locust learn
" In the domed sky to tower, stoop and turn ?
" Or shall Brihaspati [2] seek salves for ills
" From the wild herdsmen of the Deccan hills ?
" Shall tarnished tinsel strive to dazzle gold ?
" Shall before Shesh [3] the cobra's hood unfold ?
" Shall other elephants Erawat [4] show
" The gait processional, proud, solemn, slow ?
" Shall lesser godheads Shiva's self entrance
" By teaching Him the Tandva [5] step to dance ?
" Shall great Agastya [6] fear the raging brine ?
" Or shall the glow-worm teach the sun to shine ?
" Shall we the Brahman priest-hood pure as snow
" Hear sermons from the lowest of the low ?
" Get hence to-night or else ye'll know too well
" The hangman's halter or the felon's cell."
Thus Chokhamela had perforce to go
Beyond where Bhima's waters winding flow.
Far from the temples, and, though shamed, abhorred,
He yet prayed ever to the cloud-dark lord ;
And a Dipmala [7] built which still they see
Who go on pilgrimage to Pandhari.

---

[1] The eagle on which Vishnu rides.
[2] Brihaspati is the medical attendant of the gods.
[3] The snake-god.
[4] Indra's elephant.
[5] Shiva's special dance.
[6] The great sage, who angry with the sea, swallowed it up.
[7] A masonry erection for hanging lamps upon at festivals.

Once as he dined beneath a limetree's shade,
The Dark God joined him in His gems arrayed.
His wife brought curds but, as she served, some froth
Splashed on the Discus Bearer's dining cloth.
The saint rebuked her "Is it thus you treat
The lord of Vaikunth when He comes to eat?"
Then looking upwards bade a crow begone
That dropped a twig upon the necklaced one.
There passed a priest who heard and, deeply shocked,
Thought that the Mhar the absent God had mocked,
He forward sprang and, ere he could resist
He struck the saint in fury with his fist.
Then in the Bhima bathed and washed the stain
And proudly walked to pray in Vishnu's fane.
But as he prays, he sees a stain of milk.
On the God's dining cloth of priceless silk.
His cheek is swollen and the tear drops flow.
As if 'twas He had felt that cruel blow.
The Brahman saw and knew. Fear filled his breast:
"He is the saint and I a wretch confessed
"E'en as a hammer on a pearl might fall,
"I have struck him whom God loved best of all."
His pride all humbled, the priest crossed once more
To bring the saint from Bhima's further shore,
He led him back until they reached the shrine,
Where angered Vishnu had vouchsafed the sign.
And lo! the hurt cheek healed and o'er His face
Spread a smile welcoming the saint's embrace.
There close by Vishnu's side the saint found rest,
So brooks find shelter upon Ganga's breast.

The end of Chokhamela was a tragic one. In the year 1332 A. D., the Governor of Bedar impressed all the Mhars in his province in order to build a protecting wall round Mangalwedha town. Chokhamela was impressed with the others. When the work was nearing its end, a part of the unfinished wall crashed down and smothered a number of Mhar workmen. Among the victims was the subject of this article. For many years his ashes remained unhonoured under the fallen ruin. But after his death, his reputation as a saint increased so greatly, that, at last, the tailor poet Namdev received at Pandharpur a divine message to carry to Vithoba's temple the earthly remains of the pious Mhar. In obedience to it, Namdev went to Mangalwedha. But Chokhamela's bones were mingled with those of several hundred fellow workmen. At first, Namdev was at a loss to identify those which he sought. At last, placing his ear close to the ground, he heard at one spot the cry of "Vithoba, Vithoba." He then knew that the bones that lay there were Chokhamela's. Reverently he collected them, and took them to Pandharpur, where a stone erected over them, marks the spot. And there the Mhars now conduct the worship of Vishnu.

The verses which Chokhamela wrote (for he was a poet as well as a saint) have never been published. But I have been so fortunate as to collect a number of his stray stanzas. And, although he died 8 years before Chaucer's birth, Chokhamela's lines are as easily intelligible and as melodious as any in Marathi poetry. Across the Bhima river, too, may still be seen the dipmala which Chokhamela built and when the palanquin of the god Vishnu as Vithoba is monthly conveyed round the Pandharpur shrine, it stops so that floral offerings may be duly made at the saint's former dwelling place. Five hundred years after Chokhamela's death, a foreign Government, on the banks of the same river, but about a hundred odd miles up stream, built a monument of a different character, to celebrate the most brilliant victory ever gained by their arms in the East. On the 1st January, 1818, a body of Indian troops, led by British officers had, for 12 hours, with the odds at more than 30 to 1, defended the village of Koregaon against the army of Bajirao, the last Peshwa. The triumphal column, erected on the Bhima's opposite bank, shows that the bulk of those who fell in that memorable fight were soldiers of the same caste as Chokhamela. And to-day the educated members of the most unfortunate of communities regard both dipmala and column with just and equal pride. For if the one proves that, in the service of Heaven, the Deccan Mhars can, on occasion, live like saints, the other shows no less clearly that, in the service of England, they can die like heroes.

VI.

THE SAINTS OF PANDHARPUR.[1]

THE DAWN OF THE MARATHA POWER.

THE subject of my paper is the early dawn of the Maratha power. I wish, however, to preface it by some explanatory remarks. In the course of it I have carefully abstained from laying down that any particular fact is legendary and not historical. The men, whose names I shall mention, are worshipped either as divine saints or as incarnations of various deities. To hazard publicly an opinion that any of their recorded miracles never occurred might possibly give great offence.

That you may better understand the subject of this paper, I would ask you for a moment to come back with me to the year A.D. 1192. At that time Delhi was the capital of Prithvi Raj, chief of the Chohan Rajputs; Kanauj was the capital of the Rathors. South of the Vindhya Mountains a new dynasty had just emerged. One Bhillama Yadav, a Maratha chief of the same family as the rulers of Dhorasamudra in Mysore, had, after a series of battles, declared himself independent and had founded as his capital the town of Devgiri, now known as Daulatabad. In the Punjab, a foreigner had established himself. Between the Afghan cities of

[1] Lecture given before the Royal Society of Arts, London, on 17th February 1916.

Ghazni and Herat run the hills of Ghor. The wild tribes of that region had overpowered the successors of Mahmud the Ghaznivide, who more than sixty years before had raided India to sack Somnath ; and, led by a great captain, Muizzadin, better known as Mahomed Ghori, they had consolidated into a powerful kingdom, Sind, the North-Western Punjab and Eastern Afghanistan. Mahomed Ghori had, in 1191, tried to push further eastwards into India ; but he had been severely defeated by Prithvi Raj. The year A.D. 1192 was to see the Afghan's revenge. On the scene of his previous defeat he overthrew the Chohans, and on the banks of the Jumna he defeated the Rathors.

By these two victories Mahomed Ghori founded the Mussulman kingdom of Delhi, which was to last over 600 years, and in the course of his reign, most of Northern India fell a prey to his arms. The country south of the Vindhyas was not immediately affected by the success of the Ghori Afghans. For 100 years afterwards the Yadav dynasty not only endured but prospered. Thus when, in 1290, Jalaluddin Firoz Khilji became Emperor of Delhi, Ramdev Yadav, the fifth in descent from Bhillama, had been ruling over Devgiri for nineteen years. For four years more he continued to rule without any mishap, when a palace squabble in Delhi struck down his prosperity. Jalaluddin's nephew Alauddin was married to the Emperor's daughter. The marriage was unhappy, and Alauddin feared that his wife would induce her father to kill or imprison her husband. He asked for and obtained leave to collect an army to attack Chanderi. Then he passed beyond it into the Deccan, and without any warning raided

Devgiri. The raid was a complete success. The Maratha chief offered hardly any resistance and gladly paid a huge ransom. With it and the prestige of victory, Alauddin returned to Delhi, and not long afterwards murdered his uncle and became emperor in his stead. Once master of the Delhi throne, Alauddin reduced Devgiri to vassalage. His successor, Kutubuddin Mubarak, completely subdued it.

The extraordinary collapse of Devgiri was probably due to other causes than the superior physique or courage of the Mussulmans. The previous establishment of the Spaniards in the Caribbean Sea was of itself the main cause of the downfall of the Aztecs. The ferment in the mind of Montezuma more surely caused his ruin than the military skill of Cortez. In the same way the conquest of the great Rajput kingdoms of the North, and the intrusion of another religion—that of Islam—into India, upset all the previous conceptions of the Hindus. The Brahmans pronounced that the domination of the Mussulmans was foreordained to last for 30,000 years. And long before the Afghans came the Marathas had accepted them as their future conquerors. Nor did the conquest cease with the overthrow of the Yadavs. For a moment it seemed likely that the whole Deccan would turn Mussulman. From this national calamity the Maratha race was saved by the Saints of Pandharpur.

The first of these saints was Dnyandev. Although it is impossible to fix exactly the dates of any of them, we may say with some certainty that Dnyandev was a contemporary of Alauddin and of Ramdev. The story of his birth, as told by Mahipati, is as follows: The sins of the world had so increased, that Brahmadev and Shiva sought out Vishnu to consider the question. As a result of the interview Shiva took the form of Nivratti, Vishnu that of Dnyandev, and Brahmadev that of Sopana. Lastly, Laxmi assumed human shape in their sister Muktabai. The method of the incarnation was as follows: The earthly father of the three brothers and their sister was one Vithoba, a Brahman from Apegaon. His wife was one Rakhmai, the daughter of a Brahman at Alandi, a small town on the Indryani, about twelve miles north of Poona. Vithoba and Rakhmai settled at Alandi, but the married pair, although happy, were childless. In a fit of melancholy, caused by the death of his parents, Vithoba went to Benares and became a *sanyasi*, or anchorite. This was a sin on his part, for no one who has a living wife and no children should take *sanyas*. Eventually his preceptor came to hear the true facts, which Vithoba had concealed, and made him return to Alandi and once again to live with his wife. This reunion led to the birth of Nivratti, Dnyandev, Sopana and Muktabai. The return, however, of Vithoba to the life of a householder, after he had taken a vow of asceticism, offended deeply the Brahmans of Alandi. They out-casted him. And when he wished to have his son Nivratti invested with the sacred thread they refused, unless he could get the Brahmans of Paithan, a holy place on the Godaveri, to give him a letter of purification. Nivratti with his two brothers and his sister went to Paithan, asked for the letter, and at first received a flat refusal. Then the Brahmans said that if Nivratti bowed to every cow, ass, hare or dog that he met, thinking the while of Brahmadev, they would relent in his favour. Lastly, hearing Dnyandev's name, they mocked him by transferring it to a buffalo that happened to pass. Dnyandev, however, was in no way disconcerted. He placed his hand on the buffalo's head. And to show that in the sight of God no earthly distinctions mattered, he made the buffalo recite the four Vedas without an error. This miracle was soon followed by another one. He called up the ancestors of his landlord to attend the *shradh* ceremony of the latter's father in place of the Brahmans who had refused his invitation owing to the presence of his four polluted lodgers. Convinced by these two miracles, the Paithan Brahmans gave the letter of purification to Nivratti, and he was duly invested with the sacred thread. To tell the miracles of Dnyandev and his brethren would take me many hours. I shall simply relate one more, which occurred at Alandi. A certain Changdev—really an incarnation of Indra—was a Brahman of extraordinary occult power and knowledge. The allotted term of his life was only 100 years. By an original device he managed to prolong it to 1,400 years. When his 100 years were on the point of closing he disengaged his soul from his body and hid it, leaving his corpse on the ground. When Yama, the god of death, came to take away Changdev's soul, he found only an empty corpse, and after a vain search for the soul had to leave on other business. Directly Yama left, Changdev's soul came out of its hiding, re-entered his body, and started on a fresh 100 years. When he had done this fourteen times he had acquired a vast amount of experience and wisdom, and wished to try a fall with Dnyandev. Changdev did not declare open warfare. He affected to wish that Dnyandev should become his *guru*, or spiritual teacher. He wished to send him a letter to this effect, but as he could not bring himself to address Dnyandev as *tirtharup* (*i.e.*, father), he sent Dnyandev merely a blank sheet of paper. Nevertheless, Dnyandev grasped Changdev's meaning, and in reply sent him a letter of sixty-five verses. But the sense was too deep for Changdev. Unwilling to confess himself beaten, he mounted a tiger, took a snake in his hand for a whip and, followed by over one thousand pupils, he sailed through the sky until he met Dnyandev outside Alandi. Dnyandev, however, was in no way disturbed by the apparition. He mounted a wall and made it run alongside Changdev's tiger. Both man and beast were dumbfounded, and Changdev became a devout follower of Dnyandev. I may add that Changdev obtained no further extension of life. When his current one hundred years expired, Yama came again and this time carried off Changdev's soul in triumph.

The poet Namdev, to whom I shall again refer, has told in touching stanzas the death of Dnyandev. When he felt the approach of death, he asked that he might be buried at Pandharpur. But the god Krishna bade him choose Alandi as his burial place. There, amid a great company of gods and saints, Dnyandev entered alive a cave dug beneath an image of Nandi (Siva's bull), and ordered it to be closed. A golden peepul tree grew out of his tomb. His bamboo staff took root and grew into a tree. And to-day Alandi is regarded by Marathas as only second in holiness to Pandharpur.

But let us return to our main theme. Why should Dnyandev be called a Saint of Pandharpur? Pandharpur is a very old shrine in the Sholapur district, on the banks of the Bhima. It appears to have once been a shrine of Shiva ; but within historical times the worship of Shiva has been overshadowed by that of Vithal. According to Sir R. Bhandarkar, Vithal, or Vithu, is merely a Canarese corruption of Vishnu ; and at Pandharpur Vithal is regarded as a synonym of Vishnu's incarnation Krishna. Now Dnyandev was a follower of Krishna ; his books, the Dnyaneshwari and the Amritanubhav, glorify Krishna. By his talents and fame he made it the chief religious centre in the Deccan. Next, how did he save the Maratha race? To those who were drawn towards Islam, he offered another and more warmly coloured faith. Instead of the austere prophet of Arabia, he bade men look to the wondrous child of Mathura ; by holding out hopes of brighter things in a future life he enabled men better to bear their present troubles. At one time an out-caste himself, his renown as a saint proved to men of all castes that Krishna looked more to faith in him than to pure birth or sacrifice or ceremonial. Devotees of all, especially the lower, castes began to crowd to Pandharpur. One famous worshipper, Savata, was a *mali*, a gardener ; Ranka was a *kumbhar*, or potter ; Chokhamela was a *mhar*, one of the untouchable classes. Yet, according to Mahipati, he found such favour in the eyes of Vithal that one night, after the priests had mocked Chokhamela, Vithal's image descended from its shrine and, lifting Chokhamela from his bed, carried him inside the temple and placed him by its side. Nor did Pandharpur attract only Hindus. Kabir, a Mussulman weaver, was permitted to become one of Vithal's most ardent worshippers. Nor did her sex exclude Mirabai. Betrothed as a young girl in the usual Hindu way to a boy of her own caste and position, she fell in love with Krishna's image. And, resisting all and various persecutions, she became an ardent follower of the god, and eventually migrating to Dwarka, composed there the first poems ever written in Guzarathi. But when caste ties are weakened, as Dnyandev's teaching weakened them, something else must take its place. Man, a gregarious animal, wishes to associate with other men on some common basis. The usual substitutes for caste are common religion and common language. And so it followed that all those who worshipped at Pandharpur, and could speak to each other in the language of Dnyandev, and could read his poetry, became drawn to each other. In this way the Maratha race became the Maratha nation.

I would now ask you once again to turn to political history. In 1347, about fifty years after Alauddin's first assault on Devgiri, Hasan Ganga revolted against the Delhi emperor, Mahomed Tughlak, and founded what is known as the Bahmani empire; now for the first time since the conquest we hear of the Marathas. By the aid of the Maratha nobles, the revolution succeeded. They were no longer the rough country bumpkins so easily routed by Alauddin. The poetry and metaphysics of Pandharpur had enlarged their minds; they had become capable of learning military science and of proving useful allies to a great soldier. This change in the Maratha nobles is reflected in the work of the Pandharpur poet Namdev. This famous man deserves really a paper to himself; as it is, I can give him very little space. According to Mahipati, Namdev was an incarnation of Uddhav, the friend of Krishna. His parents, Damshet and Gonabai, were members of the Shimpi, or tailor caste, and lived at Pandharpur. They were childless, but in their old age Vithal took pity on them and granted them a son. He was not born in the usual way, but was found by Gonabai inside a shell that came floating down the Bhima River. Damshet and Gonabai accepted him gladly, and by means of another miracle Gonabai, although advanced in years and not his mother, was able to nurse him herself. Namdev always writes of himself as a contemporary of Dnyandev; but, as Sir R. Bhandarkar has pointed out, the difference between the Marathi of the two poets, makes this impossible. According to Sir R. Bhandarkar, Namdev lived at the close of the fourteenth century. Taking this surmise as correct, Namdev lived some years after the Bahmani empire had been founded by the aid of the Maratha nobles. He neglected entirely his tailor's business to become an ardent psalmist of the god Vithal; but whereas Dnyandev bade his readers cast out from their minds all earthly affairs, a different tendency is to be found in Namdev's verses. He advises his followers not to make vows, fasts, or pilgrimages, or to practise austerities. They will find salvation in the remembrance of Hari (*i.e.*, Vithal). If they are so unfortunate as to have worldly duties, let them perform them; but they should, during the performance, remember god always. And here follows a delightful illustration. They should act exactly like an unfaithful wife. To the outside world she appears to be attending to her husband's comforts, but inwardly she never ceases to think of her absent lover.

At the close of the fifteenth century the Bahmani empire began to break up, and in its place arose the states of Bijapur, Ahmednagar, Golconda, Berar and Bidar. These five states were always quarrelling; they were cut off from the Mussulman recruiting ground beyond the Himalayas. Thus the Marathas yearly obtained fresh opportunities of advancement, and by the sixteenth century we find Mores and Nimbalkars, Ghatges and Manes, Ghorpades and Daphles, holding high offices both in Ahmednagar and Bijapur. Indeed, it is probable that within another 200 years the Mussulman Padshahs would automatically have disappeared in favour of Hindu kings had not certain events happened beyond the Vindhyas. In 1526 Babar, King of Ferghana, successfully invaded India, and founded what is known as the Moghul Empire. In 1556 his grandson Akbar became Emperor of Delhi; and he, his grandson Shah Jehan, and his great grandson Aurangzib, never ceased to covet the southern kingdoms as former provinces of the Delhi empire. The most accessible, and therefore the first victim, was Ahmednagar, and by 1637 it had been completely annexed. It was clear that Bijapur would soon meet the same fate, and the Marathas, so far from realising their hopes of independence, seemed likely to become merely "a conscript appendage to a foreign power." Let us now see how this calamity affected the Saints of Pandharpur. In 1607, there was born at Dehu, a town fourteen miles to the north-east of Poona, one Tukaram More. He inherited a village shop, but he had no head for business. His thoughts, influenced by the sufferings of his country, turned to religion; he became bankrupt, and, leaving his wife to provide for their family as best she could, he turned for consolation to Vithoba. But the old Brahmanical opposition to saintship in inferior castes, crushed at Pandharpur, lingered at Dehu. Tukaram was forced to throw his poems into the Indryani, which passes by Dehu. Vithoba, however, befriended him, and the poems a few days later returned perfectly dry to the surface of the water. After this miracle Tukaram was hailed as a saint, and when he died at the age of forty-two or thereabouts, at Dehu, Vishnu sent his heavenly chariot to convey him to heaven. In Tukaram's works we find a distinct retreat from Namdev's position to that of the earliest saints. Nowhere have I seen any suggestion that man's duty lies in work. On the contrary, Tukaram repeats over and over again, "False is the world; Hari (*i.e.*, Vithoba) alone is real." At the same time he emphasizes the view that in the eyes of Vithoba, caste has no meaning: "God does not feel ashamed to help anyone; he seeks to comfort people of all conditions."

But if the political situation made Tukaram despair, there were two men alive at this time who saw that out of it might arise freedom. The first was a Deshasth Brahman called Narayan; he was the son of a certain Suryajipant and his wife Rambai. From his earliest days the young Brahman devoted himself to the worship, not of Vithoba, but of Ramchandra, the conqueror of Lanka, the seventh instead of the eighth incarnation of Vishnu. Nevertheless, Pandharpur can claim him as one of her saints, for, according to his biographer, Narayan received a call to Pandharpur from Vithal himself. When he went there the god informed him that Rama and Vithal were one, and commanded him to visit Pandharpur at least once a year. This command Narayan did not fail to obey. The second was a lad of amazing talents, who was growing to manhood in Poona city. His father had been one of the foremost soldiers in the service of Ahmednagar. He had tried in vain to save that kingdom, and after its fall had taken service with the king of Bijapur. The lad's mother was a descendant of the old Yadav kings of Devgiri. His parents had quarrelled and the boy grew up under the care of his mother Jijabai and an old Brahman called Dadaji Kondev. No surroundings could have been more favourable to the growth of a daring man. The Brahman repeated to the boy the old Sanskrit tales of the Indian heroes, until the latter vowed that he would be as brave as Ramchandra and as knightly as Arjuna. At the same time Jijabai told her son legends of the glory of the old Hindu kings his ancestors, and urged him to restore at least some measure of their greatness. The boy grew into a man. He first seized the forts round Poona, and then successfully defied in turn the governments of Bijapur and Delhi. His name was Shivaji Bhosle, and he is immortal as the liberator of the Maratha nation. This, however, is not the place to write of Shivaji the conqueror. I wish to show his connection with the Saints of Pandharpur. From the first Shivaji was a deeply religious man. After his successful raid on Chandrarav More, Shivaji fortified Pratapgad. It was an anxious time, as Bijapur would certainly try to avenge their officer's death. Shivaji's thoughts turned to things spiritual. He sought a preceptor to instruct him more fully in religion. By this time the young Narayan had become a renowned saint. So fervently did he worship Ramchandra that men said that he was an incarnation of Maruti, the monkey god who helped the divine hero on his southern march. And Narayan himself took the name of *Ramdas*, or slave of Rama. Shivaji heard of him, and wished to make him his *guru* or spiritual teacher, and went to see him at Chaphal, where he had built a temple to his favourite god. But Ramdas hid himself and Shivaji sought him everywhere in vain. At last Shivaji vowed that he would not touch food until he had seen the saint. Then Ramdas relented. He sent him a metrical letter exhorting him to restore the Hindu religion and to clear the country of its Mussulman oppressors. The next day Shivaji and Ramdas met. The king, delighted with the letter, was still more pleased with the saint. He would not, however, make Ramdas his *guru* without a test. He ordered him, so runs a story, to fetch a *ser* of tigress' milk. Such a task was nothing to Ramdas. He went at once into the forest, sought out a tigress with cubs, milked her, and brought back the milk to the king. From this time on Ramdas was the constant companion and spiritual guide of the king. His influence was wise and kindly. While he taught Shivaji the duties of kingship, and the divine task which lay before him of freeing his countrymen, he at the same time bade him not to be over stern, to speak no harsh words, not to cherish his anger, and not to act unjustly in any matter. And Shivaji's career shows this teaching. He gave no mercy to Afzul Khan, the Bijapur general, but he treated his beaten army with the utmost consideration. Shivaji would have killed Aurangzib without scruple; but when Abaji Sondev captured, and sent as a present to the king, the beautiful daughter-in-law of Mulana Ahmad—the Mussulman governor of Kalyan—Shivaji sent her home again to her relations with all respect. In spite of his influence over Shivaji, Ramdas was wise enough not to seek to guide his campaigns. Unlike Peter the Hermit, Ramdas did not wish both to inspire and to lead a crusade. When Shivaji heard of the approach of Afzul Khan, he asked Ramdas' advice. The saint replied that he could not advise. Shivaji should pray for guidance to Bhavani, the goddess of Pratapgad. The saint knew that the king's fertile brain would, if left to itself, devise the proper measures. But when the king grew vain of his victories, Ramdas did not hesitate to rebuke him. Once the king and the saint were watching the building of Samangad fort. Thousands of men were at work, all paid by the royal treasury. The king let fall some remark that showed his pride that he was the source of their livelihood. "That," replied Ramdas, "is but a small part of your great work." He then bade some workmen split open a boulder close by. In the centre was a cavity half filled with water, in the water was a frog. "O, king," said Ramdas, "who but you could have made a hole in the centre of the stone, placed a frog in it and provided it with water." The king was confused, asked the saint's forgiveness, and admitted that it was alike God who had kept alive the frog, and God who cared for the needs of the workers at Samangad.

Now let us sum up the work of the Saints of Pandharpur. In the first place, they drew the thoughts of the Marathas away from Islam. Secondly, they created a centre at once literary and religious, and thus made of the race a nation. Thirdly, by their doctrines and writings they improved and enlarged the minds of the Maratha leaders, so that they became the indispensable servants of their conquerors. Fourthly, by belittling caste, they united the Maratha nation, and thus made the way smooth for the coming of a national hero. And lastly, when that hero came, great beyond human expectation—I had almost said human imagination—they made him better than great. They made him modest and just, pure minded and humane.

VII.

THE SATURDAY PALACE.

THE Shanwar Wada or Saturday Palace is the most historic building in the Deccan. Its first stone was laid on the 10th January 1730 A.D., and it was completed towards the end of 1731 A.D. It derives its name of the Saturday Palace from the coincidence that its Vastushanti (or the sacrifice to the Earth spirit by the burial of a live Mang beneath the projected site) occurred on a Saturday. And its foundation stone was also laid on a Saturday.

Fully to understand the history of the Shanwar Wada one must go back to the year 1640. About that time there lived in Poona—then a petty township—a wild, neglected boy who spent half of his time in dreaming of military exploits and the other half in listening to religious poems and indulging in wild fits of ascetic mortification. His father Shahaji Bhosle was at first a captain in the service of the Musalman king of Ahmadnagar. After the fall of that monarchy, Shahaji took service with the king of Bijapur. The boy's mother was one Jijabai Yadav, the daughter of Lakhaji Yadav, the head of one of the most aristocratic families in all southern India. His ancestors had been in the 12th century Emperors of Devgiri and the boy's mother never ceased to impress upon her son, that some day she wished to see him restore the former glories of her ancient line. Shahaji Bhosle's duties kept him for years together at the Bijapur Court. He was thus forced to leave Jijabai to look after his son and his Deccan estates in Poona. The absence of paternal control gave the wild boy every chance to turn his dreams into realities. Gathering round him a band of half-naked hillmen, he seized the hillforts in the neighbourhood of Poona. Success harmonized his religious enthusiasm with his earthly ambitions. And he believed himself and he convinced his followers that he had been appointed by the Goddess Bhavani to free Southern India from the yoke of the Musalman. Boundless ardour, tireless strength, and an infinite knowledge of the country-side were combined with the usual courage and capacity of a great captain. Success followed success in almost monotonous sequence and when he died in 1680, still in the prime of manhood, he had conquered a territory as large as Spain. His name was Shivaji Bhosle. His son Sambhaji all but lost the Empire which his father had won. And nothing but the internal struggles of the Mogal princes enabled Sambhaji's son Shahu to become king of the Marathas. In 1708, however, an event occurred which was to change the whole history of India. A Chitpavan Brahman called Balaji Vishwanath was forced to flee from his home in Shrivardhan near Janjira. He took refuge in the territories of king Shahu and accepted a petty clerkship under the ancestor of the very Sardar Purandhare, whose house now stands opposite the Shanwar Wada. So remarkable were Balaji's abilities that in six years he had risen from a clerkship to the post of Peshwa or prime minister. And when he died in 1720, full of honours, he bequeathed the post of prime minister to his son Bajirao, who held it for no less than 20 years. And now we must turn to the Shanwar Wada. Ten years after Bajirao had succeeded to his father's office and after his talents had in turn brought to him even greater wealth and fame than that they had brought his father, Bajirao decided to build for himself a fitting residence. And it was characteristic of the ambitions which the family probably cherished even then, that he chose for his new palace* the site of the very house where Shivaji Bhosle had passed his youth. King Shahu made no sign of the repugnance which he felt until Bajirao began to erect in front of the palace strong fortifications. The king then sent him a message begging him to desist on the ground that as the palace faced northward, the erection of a fortified gate might annoy and frighten the Emperor of Delhi. Bajirao took the hint and discontinued the work. When Bajirao died in 1740, he was succeeded in his office by his son Balaji. And in 1750, when king Shahu died, the new prime minister made a coup d' ètat. He shut up king Shahu's heir Ram Raja in Satara fort, and became the *de facto* ruler of the Maratha Empire. And one of his first acts as ruling prince was the completion of the fortifications round the Shanwar Wada.

I shall now ask my readers to accompany me round the Shanwar Wada going eastwards from the large gate. The first thing to notice is a small gate in the northern wall. This is known as Mastani's gate. And the story connected with it has a touch of romance. On one occasion Bajirao had gone into the heart of Central India with a large Maratha army to rescue Bundelcund

* The Rang Mahal, where Shivaji lived, stood on the spot where Bajirao built his elephant lines or ambarkhana.

from a Mogal attack. While the Maratha forces were thus heavily engaged, another Mogal army penetrated into Haidarabad. The Nizam asked for Maratha aid. But the king without either minister or army did not know how to meet his appeal. The dilemma of the king came to the knowledge of Chimnaji Appa, Bajirao's younger brother. Chimnaji at once offered to raise a force of volunteers and take them with him to assist the Nizam. The king pleased at the boy's spirit accepted the offer. And Chimnaji and his volunteers did so well that he drove the Mogals back towards Delhi and captured their general's camp. Among the spoils was a beautiful dancing girl called Mastani, whom the Mogal commander Shahazat Khan had brought with him to beguile the tedium of the campaign. Mastani tried when captured to take poison. But Chimnaji prevented her and took her back with him to Poona. There he presented her to his elder brother, who fell deeply in love with her. The acute Mastani saw the effect of her charms and refused to become the minister's mistress, unless he promised her to give an equal share in his estate to any son whom she might bear him. The minister would have bought her consent on any terms. He made the promise and kept it. And their son Samsher Bahadur lived to become a wealthy and distinguished noble. He fell at Panipat. To Mastani, Bajirao assigned a suite in his new palace and the door which led into it is the door still called Mastani's gate. In front of it is a Musalman tomb believed by the public to be hers.

In the Eastern wall there are two doors, the first of which is known as the Jambhul gate, because a large

Jambhul tree grew near it. The second is known as the Ganpati gate because of the image of Ganpati at the door. The image played a large part in the family history of the Peshvas, because they were all devout worshippers of that particular God. But the gate itself has a sinister history. Balaji Bajirao, as I have said, succeeded his father in 1740, and made his famous coup d' ètat in 1750. The years between 1750 to 1779, Balaji spent in pushing in every direction the Maratha arms. At last the Mogal Empire began to totter to its fall. But its decline brought in its train a new danger. With all their faults, the Mogal Emperors had successfully closed the North-West passes against the barbarians of Central Asia. Harassed from every side by the Maratha advance, the Mogals withdrew their troops from the Hindu-Kush to Hindusthan. The barbarians from beyond the mountains were not slow to grasp the situation ; and in 1739 the Persian King Nadir Shah invaded India and sacked Delhi. The Maratha armies mobilized with a view to drive him from India, but no conflict occurred. The Persian army left with its plunder and shortly after they had recrossed the border, Nadir Shah was assassinated. The Persian kingdom fell on his death into disorder, but an Afghan soldier in his service called Ahmadshah Abdali, saved part of his Empire from the wreck and founded the modern kingdom of Afghanistan.

In 1760, Ahmadshah led an Afghan army into India. Balaji sent his cousin Sadashivrao and his son Vishvasrao to oppose the Afghans. But the Maratha army was defeated with fearful slaughter on the plain of Panipat near Delhi. Among the killed were Sadashivrao and

Vishvasrao. The news of their deaths overwhelmed the Peshwa and he died shortly afterwards among the Parvati temples. His successor was his second son Madhavrao I. Although only 16, such was his capacity that he succeeded in restoring the Maratha fortunes. The Afghans were driven beyond the mountains and had Madhavrao I lived, the whole of India would have been ruled from the Shanwar Wada. But this was not to be. For in the 28th year of his age this able young prince died at Theur of consumption. At the time of Balaji's death, Madhavrao I's accession was opposed by Balaji's younger brother Raghunathrao. Madhavrao I proved too strong for the pretender. But on his nephew's death Raghunathrao's hopes again rose. Between him, however, and the throne stood Madhavrao I's younger brother Narayanrao. On the first opportunity, therefore, Raghunathrao compassed the boy prince's murder. His arts corrupted a band of guardsmen led by one Sumersing. They came to the palace and clamoured loudly for their arrears of pay. Allowed to approach the Ganpati gate, they suddenly forced it and rushing through it into the inner apartments hacked the young Peshwa to pieces. The murder, however, brought its perpetrators no reward. Narayanrao's widow gave birth to a posthumous son and the country chivalrously rallied to the cause of the queen-mother and the little prince. Raghunathrao had to flee the country and Nana Phadnavis, a Brahman of great ability, assumed the Government in the name of Narayanrao's son, who is known to history as Madhavrao II. Nana Phadnavis lived in a house on the site of which the New English School now stands, that is to say immediately to the south of the south-eastern corner of the Shanwar Wada. The mother of Madhavrao II, Gangabai, resided with her son in the Shanwar palace. But scandal* whispered that the regent's interviews with the widowed queen were not only those required by the affairs of State. She, however, did not long survive her husband's murder and from the time of her death onwards Nana Phadnavis ruled the Maratha Empire as absolute autocrat. Raghunathrao, who had died in 1784, had left a son called Bajirao after his grandfather. This young prince Nana Phadnavis kept a state prisoner in Junnar. As he and his cousin Madhavrao II grew to manhood, the two young men became interested in each other and began to write each other letters, unknown to the regent. At last their correspondence was discovered and the regent spoke with extreme sharpness to Madhavrao II. The boy king's spirit, already broken by the jealous watch which his minister kept over him, gave way altogether. He fell ill of fever and on the 25th October 1795, threw himself either deliberately or in a delirium from his window at the top of the palace into the court-yard. As he fell, his thigh struck the central fountain jet and was broken. The death of this promising young ruler brings me naturally to the door on the southern side of the Shanwar Wada. For through that door the bodies of the dead Madhavrao and of all those who ever died within the palace walls were carried to the burning ground. It might be thought more natural that a dead prince should be carried in state through the main entrance. But the Hindus have a good

* Mr. Rajvade has collected evidence to show that the scandal had no foundation in fact.

reason for not doing so. They believe that if a corpse were carried out through the front door, the dead man's ghost would return through it at the earliest opportunity and haunt its former dwelling place. To avoid such a contingency Hindu houses have a back door, through which the dead are taken to their last resting place. After the funeral procession has passed through the back door, it is carefully closed. Thus when the ghost seeks to return by the road along which it accompanied its former tenement it cannot do so. For the back door is, as I have said, kept shut. And the ghost does not know the way through the front door.

Let us, however, achieve what the ghost cannot, and let us enter by the southern gate of the Shanwar Wada and try to picture ourselves how it looked in the days of the Peshwas. On the central mound stood the main palace. It was six stories high and had four large and several smaller court-yards. The four larger court-yards had fountains, and on one of them, as I have said, Madhavrao II fell, shattering his thigh. The four main court-yards were known as the Granary Court, the Dancing Court, the Kitchen Court and the Sweetmeat Court. In the palace there were no less than seven great halls of audience. The first was known as the Gokak Hall, because its walls were hung with toys made in Gokak. The second was known as the Nach or Dancing hall, because here the dancing girls beguiled the tedium of the Peshvas' leisure hours. The third was known as the Mirror Hall and about it the chronique scandaleuse of the early 19th century had an amusing story to tell. When Madhavrao II died, his cousin Bajirao II was the only surviving descendant of Bajirao I and, in spite of Nana Phadnavis' opposition, he succeeded to the vacant throne. The young prince was skilled in arms; and deeply read in Sanskrit lore. His face was handsome and his stature commanding. Like Charles II he might have been a great king if he would. But like his Stuart prototype the will was lacking. The time that might have been spent in affairs of state were spent in enjoying the charms of dancing girls or in winning the favours of his nobles' wives. And this brings me back to the Mirror Hall. It derived its name from the thousand mirrors which covered its ceiling, walls and floor. And the story runs that Bajirao II offered two beautiful pieces of jewelry to two highly placed ladies of his Court, on condition that they walked unrobed through the Mirror Hall to take them. The prince promised to keep the matter a dead secret and the ladies tempted by the jewelry agreed to the condition. One of them, ashamed to be seen in the garb of Eve, walked across the room to fetch the prize in the attitude of the Venus dei Medici. The other, thinking of nothing but the jewel to be gained, walked as unconcernedly as if she had been clad in ermine. The ladies received their rewards. But the prince did not keep the secret. The story became the property of the Poona public. And the court-wits gave nicknames to each one of the two ladies. The nicknames may be translated as "Crouching Kate" and "Susan Straight."*

The fourth hall was the Kacheri Diwan Khana. It was here that the Peshwas received their Ministers and the Ambassadors of foreign powers. This hall is one which as a peculiar interest for us. In the south of

* The Marathi names are Vakdi Veni and Saral Salu.

India, there had through many centuries existed an ancient Hindu dynasty who ruled over the kingdom of Mysore. It had survived through many vicissitudes and had resisted the attacks of Bijapur by arms and those of the Mogals by diplomacy. At last owing to circumstances too lengthy to be related here, the dynasty and the kingdom alike became the prey of a trooper in the royal service. His name was Haider Ali. On his death in 1782, he left to his successor Tipu Sultan, a disciplined army and vast resources. Before the common danger from this new power, the long antagonism between the English and the Marathas vanished. On the 1st June 1790 the Peshwa, Mr. Malet, on behalf of the Bombay Government, and the Haidarabad envoy, on behalf of the Nizam, signed in the Kacheri Diwan Khana the triple alliance, which despatched the armies that forced the Sultan of Mysore to the peace of Seringapatam. A picture of this incident, drawn by the artist Wales, in preserved in H. E. the Governor's palace at Ganeshkhind. A fifth hall was known as the Ivory Hall, because of its ivory ornamentation. A sixth was called the Ganesh Diwan Khan, wherein Ganpati, the tutelary God of the Peshwas, was on Ganesh Chaturthi (Bhadrapad 4th) his birthday worshipped with fitting splendour. The seventh hall was known as Narayanrao's Hall. And it was here that Narayanrao Peshwa fell beneath the swords of his assassins.

At the present moment not a vestige of the old palace remains. It was burnt to the ground early in 1827. So we can readily walk across the inner space back to the main gate from which we started. The heavy wooden doors are provided with solid iron spikes. These illustrate a curious stage in the everlasting conflict between the attack and the defence in warfare. Some early general discovered in remote times that the stoutest gate would yield if a war elephant charged it head first. Afterwards it occurred to some commandant of a fortress that, if sharp spikes were fastened to the gate, the war elephant could not be induced to charge it effectively. Then some Indian Demetrios met the difficulty by tying a dead camel to his war elephant's head. The spikes entered the camel's body and the gates yielded to the shock of the charge. Finally, however, some Eastern Vauban defeated the war elephant by building narrow winding lanes as approaches to fortress gates. Into them the war elephant could not enter. The main gate of the Shanwar Wada not being exposed to attack illustrates the earlier stage of fortification. It has only spikes but is not protected by a narrow approach. Above it is the drum room where the Peshwa kept the war drums used by his guardsmen. But the verandah in front of it has a tragic interest of its own. In 1767 Malhar Rao Holkar, the founder of the great ruling house of Indore, died. He was succeeded by Tukoji Holkar, who, in turn, died on August 15th, 1797. He left two legitimate and two illegitimate sons. Of the two legitimate sons, the elder Khanderao was an imbecile. The younger Malhar Rao was murdered by the orders of his rival Sindia shortly after his accession. This crime enabled Sindia to occupy the whole of the Indore territories, and Tukoji's two illegitimate sons Vithuji and Yeshwantrao fled their country. Deprived of their inheritance they turned brigands. Yeshwantrao defied all efforts to seize him but Vithuji was defeated and taken. He was brought to Poona into the presence of Bajirao II. The latter sentenced the disinherited prince to be dragged about the streets at an elephant's foot until he died. The Peshwa then seated himself in the verandah of the drum room and watched his wretched victim being dragged to his death through the gate below. After Vithuji's death, his body was burnt near Holkar's bridge which derives its name from this episode. His widow committed sati on the spot on which Holkar's temple now stands.

The cruelty of the Peshwa brought him abundant retribution. Yeshwantrao, Vithuji's brother, who had many of the qualities of a great captain, succeeded in collecting a large force in order to avenge his brother. Evading Sindia's troops he marched on Poona. As he advanced his army grew and when the armies of the rival powers met between Loni and Hadapsar, Yeshwantrao was completely victorious. Bajirao fled to the English in Bombay, and with their assistance he recovered his throne. But his allies, who knew the dangers in front of them and who afterwards in his defence fought the battles of Assaye, Laswari and Deeg, made the Peshwa pay handsomely for their assistance. This offended Bajirao II, and although he signed the treaty of Bassein on the 31st December 1802, he never afterwards ceased to regret having done so. These regrets found expression in intrigues with his former enemies against his former friends. At last an attack on the Resident, Mr. Mountstuart Elphinstone, led to the battles of Kirkee, Koregaon and Ashta, and the final downfall of the dynasty who so long had lived and ruled in the Shanwar palace.

From the foregoing sketch it will, I think, be seen that the Shanwar Wada is intimately connected with the entire history of the Maratha nation. On its site, a genius not inferior to Frederick dreamed of successes even more dazzling than his. Into its gates Maratha captains brought back cannon and standards torn from the armies of England, Afghanistan and Portugal. In its vanished chambers were conceived alliances which shook thrones by the Jamna and upon the heights above the Cauvery. From its court-yards set forth the squadrons who planted the Maratha banner on the walls of Attock and on the towers of Badami. Its halls once smiled on the loves of Bajirao I and on the revels of Bajirao II. Its terraces once whispered a romance similar to that which Dumas wove round the names of Anne of Austria and of Cardinal Mazarin. Its rooms once witnessed a crime as black as that of Ravaillac and a tragedy as sombre as that which clouded the youth and childhood of the unhappy Duke of Reichstadt.

> Yes, this was once Ambitions' airy hall
> The dome of thought, the palace of the soul
>
> . . . .
>
> The gay recess of wisdom and of wit.
> And Passion's lust, that never brooked control.
> Can all saint, sage, or sophist ever writ,
> People this lonely tower, this tenement refit ?

VIII.

THE FEAST OF LANTERNS.

DASERA has gone with its Shami tree celebrations and its Simolanghan ceremonies and now in the same month—that of Ashwin—has come Divali with its crackers and its three days' holidays. Dasera falls on the 10th day of the bright half of Ashwin. Divali lasts from the 13th of the dark half of Ashwin to the 2nd day of the bright half of Kartik and thus, in the countries north of the Narmada, where the Sanvat year founded by King Kanishka is in force, bridges over the old and the new years of the Hindu cycle.

To those of us who profit by the holiday it may not be uninteresting to enquire why the magistrates' and judges' courts are closed and why small boys deem themselves privileged to discharge squibs and catherine wheels under the noses of the magistrates' and judges' horses.

Divali is the abbreviated form of Dipawali, or the line of lamps which marks the festival, and this is the tale to be found in the Sanatkumar Sanhita of the month of Kartik as told by Sanatkumar, the fourth son of Brahma, to the 60,000 Falkhilya Rishis.

One day King Yama, lord of the Infernal Regions, asked his messengers whether they had ever felt pity for any of the countless lives which at his command they had transported from earth to hell. The leader of the messengers replied "O King Yama, once we felt pity and it was in this wise. In Hastinapura there dwelt a king called Hansaraj. One day when out hunting he lost his way and eventually sat down in despair, thinking to die of thirst. Suddenly he heard in the distance the cry of a crane which gave him the hope that not far away lay water. He made his way in the direction of the cry and came to a lake where some Kolis were fishing. They told him that he had reached the lands of his feudatory vassal King Sanwarta whose capital, Nagawan, was only a *kos* away. Refreshed by the waters of the lake, Hansaraj reached Nagawan and there was entertained with such honour as befits a vassal to show to his overlord. That night as he lay in Sanwarta's palace King Hansaraj awoke. He rose and looked out and saw a woman enter the palace door with a pen in her hand. He spoke to her and asked her who she was. But she passed on without heeding him. He then went to the door and sat down and awaited her return. When she came he seized her and again asked her who she was, threatening that unless she answered him he would slay her. She spoke and said "I am the Goddess of Life, Jivantika, and had you not been a pious king I should have killed you and shall do so still unless you let me go."

Now King Hansaraj was a Kshatriya prince and he feared neither man nor god nor devil, so he held Jivantika firm and he made her tell her story. And she said* "O King, I am the Goddess of Life* and on the 6th day

* In proof of the truth of this I may mention that from the 5th to the 15th day after a child's birth, there are kept near its cot a pen, inkstand and a penknife. These are for the use of Jivantika.

after the birth of every living thing I go and write on its forehead the fate allotted to it according to the action of its former life, and I have just inscribed on the 6th day old child of King Sanwarta its life's story." Then spoke King Hansaraj "What have you written?" Jivantika said, "I have written that four days after its marriage it will die of a serpent bite." Then Hansaraj let her go and went back to Hastinapura. But for grief at the sorrow which awaited his vassal Sanwarta and his little son, King Hansaraj had no rest. And at last he ordered his minister to build in the bed of the Yamuna river a mighty castle. And the castle was so built that it had but one door. And that closed, there was no room for even an ant to enter. And thither King Hansaraj took his vassal Sanwarta and made him dwell there with his son. When the boy was sixteen years old, King Hansaraj married him to a princess whose horoscope suited his own. And on the 4th day after the marriage King Hansaraj sat with the boy and with them were doctors and soothsayers to defend him against the serpent. And, O King Yama, we your messengers felt pity for the boy whom you had ordered us to slay. But we were servants of the Word and so I entered the nose of King Hansaraj as a mosquito and he squeezed me out and I fell to earth and took a snake's form and stung the son of Sanwarta. And the cunning of the doctors and the charms of the soothsayers availed him nothing for he died instantly. And O King Yama, we your messengers sorrowed exceedingly; so tell us, we pray you, how man may avert so sudden a death. Then King Yama said "Let those on whose foreheads sudden death is written, place on the 13th Vadya

Ashwin outside their door and facing the south a lamp with a black wick and perchance I may spare them." Thus, as no man knows what is written on his forehead, there is on the 13th of the black half of Ashwin placed outside each Hindu household a lamp made of earth or of wheat flour and with a black wick and it is turned to the south that King Yama when he sees it may take pity.* And on the following day, the 14th of the 2nd half of Ashwin, water libations are poured to King Yama in his 14 names--Yama ; Dharmraja, Lord of Religion ; Mritya or Death ; Antak or Ender ; Vaivasvat ; Kal or Time ; Sarvabhutkshaya or Killer of all Life ; Oudumbar ; Dadhna or Destroyer ; Nila or Dark One ; Parmeshthi or Mighty One ; Vrikodar or wolf-bellied ; Chitra or Picture ; and Chitragupta or the Recording Angel.

But the 14th day of the dark half of Ashwin has a sanctity of its own and that a double one. The common story told is that it is the anniversary of the god Vishnu's fight with the demon Narkasur. After killing him Vishnu early in the morning entered his city and the people illuminated it in his honour and the women went to meet him and waved lighted lamps round his head. And so on the 14th Ashwin Vadya a married woman, in each Brahmin's household, rises at 3 a.m.,

*Lamps are ordinarily never turned to the south. The only other occasion that a lamp is so placed is when a man or woman dies, ashes are placed on the spot and on them is put a lamp turned to the south. It is also to be noted that the lamp to Yama must be placed outside the house. The great thing is not to let him in. In this connection there is an amusing Gujerati saying "Doshimari jai to phikar nathi pan Jam (Yama) ghar joy jay." "It does not matter a straw about the old hag dying except that Death gets to know the inside of that house."

draws a square in the entrance room, places a low stool in the square and close to the stool sets cups of spices and scented oil and on each side of it a lighted brass lamp. The head of the house then sits on the stool and the barber rubs him down with rice-flour, spices and oil and anoints his topknot with cocoanut milk. Then he goes to the yard, traces a square facing the east, bathes on a high wooden stool and putting on a waist cloth and turban stands in front of the house. His wife then marks his forehead with red powder and a few rice grains, hands him a cocoanut and waves the lighted lamp in front of his face. For this was the women's welcome to the victorious Vishnu.

But the authority which I have already quoted gives another story. Once there lived a king by name Bali, or the Mighty, whose qualities and austerities had made him master of the earth and who coveted India's throne. Now it is known that he who can perform 100 Ashwa medhas or horse-sacrifices has the right to oust Indra therefrom and King Bali had already performed 99. Indra in despair appealed to Vishnu and Vishnu in pity entered the womb of the wife of Kashyapa, the Rishi, and was born in his 5th incarnation of Waman or the Dwarf. As a tiny shrunken human atom Vishnu approached the throne of King Bali and craved a boon. King Bali asked what it should be and the Dwarf replied that he wanted as much land as he could cover in three strides. The wicked king laughingly consented. Then Vishnu grew until he filled the whole horizon and the same day he covered in his first stride the earth. On the next day in his 2nd stride he covered the heavens and on the 3rd day with his 3rd stride he stamped King

Bali into Hell. King Bali then in turn asked for a boon, which was granted, and the boon was that Bali should be worshipped for three days in the year and these days are the 14th and 30th (called Amavashya) of the latter half of Ashwan and the first day of Kartik Sudha, for they are the anniversaries of the days on which Vishnu triumphed. And on the 1st of these three days the women light the lamps and take them to the stables and the grooms and cowherds wave them round the heads of the horses and cattle repeating the couplet "Ida Pida Javo, Baliche Raj yevo" (Fly away fly away trouble and pain, Bali's kingdom come again). The second day of Bali's three days is the children's day, probably because of Vishnu's diminutive stature. Should they fight then there will be war in the land. Should they cry there will be sorrow. If any of them armed with a stick mounts a horse, then a neighbouring kingdom will be conquered. If a child tries to light a lamp and fails, then there will be cholera in the capital. If he goes and hides his food, then there will be a famine.

So to keep the children pleased the kings in olden time distributed toys. Modern kings have no doubt other uses for their money. But the little ones are no losers. For their parents on the mornings of the last day of Ashwin put toys outside the hall door to simulate the king's presents. The 3rd of King Bali's days is, as I have said, the 1st day of the Sanvat year and the Banias open new accounts and worship their books. But besides being sacred to King Bali the 1st of Kartik Shudha has a tale of its own. On this day Shankar and Parvati gambled, and the wife won from the husband the three worlds. Then he went away sorrowing until he met Kartik Swami, his son. To him he told his misfortune and Kartik Swami induced his step-mother to play with him and recovered from her his father's possession. So on this day Hindus play draughts from 6 a.m. to 9 a.m., and as the gods set the bad example, good men may on this day gamble without reproach. Nay, they may even, according to my authority, turn to beauty fair and frail, and yet bear no stain upon their character.

Now we have come to the last day and leaving King Bali and his woes we must return to King Yama. It appears that for many days before the 2nd of Kartik his sister Yamuna had been pressing his majesty to dine at her house. But like the modern district officer, he was far too busy with his office work to accept. What with sending out his messengers to pick off human beings, recording their sins as they arrived, and fitting them out with careers when they re-entered human shapes, he had absolutely no time to spare. Eventually, however, she on the 2nd day of the bright half of Kartik succeeded in overcoming his scruples. She took him off to dinner, fed him daintly, oiled and scented him like an Assyrian bull and finally lighting a niranjan, or little brass lamp, waved it round his head. She then begged him that in future anyone who dined with his sister on that day and gave her presents should be happy through the year. King Yama took the hint and loaded her with jewels and the custom now prevails that brothers should on 2nd Kartik visit their sisters. The latter wave lamps, round their heads and receive presents and the day is therefore called the "Bhaubij" or "the brother's second" and the gift given is called the Ovalni or the gift of waving. But my authority goes on to explain that he who is on a journey and has sisters may acquire equal merit by merely reading the Sanat Kumar Sanhita. So I think that if I were a Hindu and blessed with many sisters I should as Kartik Shud 2nd approached go on a long journey and on Bhaubij day I should sit and read my author. Thus the claim of religion would be satisfied and the cost of the presents saved.

IX.

A DECCAN NURSERY TALE.

THE FALSE PRINCE.[1]

ONCE upon a time there was a town called Atpat. In it there reigned a King who had no son. At last his Queen sent for a midwife and said 'O dear, dear midwife, I want you to get me secretly a little baby boy only just born. If you get him for me I shall give you great wealth.' The midwife promised to get the baby boy for the Queen and then began to search all over Atpat. As it happened a poor Brahman woman, who lived in the town, was expecting to become a mother. The midwife went to her house and said 'Lady, lady, directly you feel the birth pains coming on, send for me. As you are poor I shall attend you through your confinement and charge you nothing.' The poor Brahman woman agreed. Thereafter the midwife went to the Queen and said 'Lady, lady, I have found in the city a poor Brahman woman who has been *enceinte* only just over a month. All her symptoms lead me to think that she will give birth to a boy. So very secretly get a subterranean passage built from your palace to her house and in a day or two start the report that you are *enceinte.* Directly the boy is born I shall bring him to you. The Queen

[1]. For the rest of the series of Deccan Nursery Tales see my book "Deccan Nursery Tales" (Macmillan & Co.)

was overjoyed at the midwife's promise and after a few days she gave out that she was about to become a mother. At the same time she stuffed a quantity of clothes round her waist so as to keep up the pretence. She had the subterranean passage built and when the proper number of months had passed, she began to make ready for her expected confinement. In the meantime the Brahman woman felt the birth pains coming on and called the midwife. The midwife send word that she was coming and at once ran off and told the Queen to pretend also to be in great pain. Then she went to the Brahman woman's house and said 'Lady, lady, as this is your first child, I must blindfold you. If I do, all will be well. If not, I cannot answer for the consequences.' With these words she blindfolded the poor Brahman woman. In a little time she gave birth to a baby boy. The midwife handed the boy to a slave girl who carried it by the subterranean passage to the Queen's room. Then the midwife took a kitchen roller [1] and tied it to a broom and placed it in the Brahman woman's lap. Then the midwife unbandaged her eyes and said to her "You have only given birth to a broom and a kitchen roller." The poor Brahman woman grew very sad but, although she did not believe the midwife, she resigned herself to her fate. The midwife ran off to the palace. There the news had spread that the Queen had been confined and every one was coming in to look at and admire the newly born baby boy. In the meantime the Brahman woman resolved that every Friday through Shravan she would worship the God-

---

[1]. Warwanta is a roller used for pounding chillies and other spices.

dess Jivati [1] and would pray, 'O Goddess Jivati, mother of all, please, please take care of my little baby boy wherever he be'. Then she would scatter rice on the ground in the hope that they might be blown away and so perhaps fall on her little son's head. And she left off wearing fine green clothes and green bangles and she would never go under arches made of the karle tree, nor would she step over water in which rice had been cleaned. In course of time the false baby prince grew to be a man and when the King of Atpat died, he succeeded him on the throne. One day he went out for a walk and passed the Brahman woman. She had just bathed and was sitting in her garden, watching her vegetables. Directly the prince's eye lit on her, he fell in love with her and determined to visit her that very night. After dark he set out towards her house. Near her door were tied a cow and its calf. As he came, he trod by accident on the calf's tail. The calf bellowed with the pain and said to its mother 'Who is that sinner who has trod on my tail?' The cow answered 'Is it likely that a man who falls in love with his own mother, will care a straw whether he treads on your tail?' When the prince heard this, he stopped and turned back. On reaching the palace he asked leave of the Queen

---

1. Jivati is the same as Jivantika. She is the Goddess who preserves the lives of little childern and writes their future destinies. That she may do this she is worshipped on the 5th and 6th days after a child's birth, and a pen, paper, and inkstand and open knife are placed near its cradle. Satvi is the Goddess who kills little children. She is also worshipped to appease her wrath at the same time as Jivati. The vow taken by the Brahman woman is the vow peculiar to the worship of Jivati, except that of not stepping over water in which rice has been cleaned. No Brahman woman will ever do this, if she can help it.

mother to go to Benares. The Queen consented and the prince set out on his journey. As he went, he stopped at the house of a Brahman. Now that Brahman had had several sons, but they had all died on the 5th or 6th day after their birth. And on the very day that the prince came the Brahman's last child was five days old. The prince lay down to sleep in the Brahman's door-way and then a marvellous thing happened. In the middle of the night the Goddess Satvi came to snatch away the Brahman's child, when she saw the prince lying in the door-way. She called out in a loud voice 'Who is this cursed wretch who blocks my path?' The Goddess Jivati replied 'Prayers have been offered to me for the safety of the boy sleeping there and I shall not let you pass over him.' Now the Brahman and his wife were sitting up in sadness by their child's cradle. For it was the 5th day and they expected that he would be snatched from them. They heard the talk between Satvi and Jivati. And immediately afterwards they saw the two Goddesses go away together. Next morning the Brahman fell at the prince's feet and thanking him for saving his child's life, pressed him to remain with them. The prince agreed to stay another day. But the following morning he started again for Benares. When the time came for him to go to Gaya,[1] he went there and offered the rice cakes. Suddenly two out-stretched

1. The Gayavarjan is the rite performed by persons who have lost their father. The Kashi-yatra consists of three pilgrimages (i) to Kashi or Benares, (2) to Prayag or Allahabad, (3) to Gaya. At Gaya, the pilgrims who have lost their father perform a special memorial ceremony called the Gayawarjan. The cause of the miracle was the fact that the prince's real father, as will be seen later, was still alive. The prince, therefore, had no business to perform the Gayawarjan and the God Vishnu protested.

hands came out of the ground to take them. The prince asked the priests the meaning of this strange happening. They said 'Return to your home; summon all your subjects, both men and women, and give them dinner. Then you will know the meaning of the miracle." The prince returned home wondering greatly. He first worshipped water from the Ganges river with great pomp and circumstance. He then issued an order that no kitchen-fire should be lit throughout all Atpat, and that every dweller there should come and dine in the Royal Palace. Now it so happened that it was a Friday, the day on which the Brahman woman used to worship Jivati. She was sore perplexed and sent the following message to the prince: 'I have vowed to worship Jivati and I worship her with many rites. Unless you permit me to observe them, I cannot come to dinner.' The prince consented. The Brahman woman first neaped over every spot on the road where rice water had been thrown and only then passed over it. She wore no green bangles. And she refused to pass under the arches made of Kàrle branches. And as she went, she prayed beneath her breath 'O Goddess Jivati, keep my son well and happy wherever he be.' At last the feast began. Every kind of splendid dish was served on leaves to the assembled villagers. The prince himself handed round the ghee. As he served it, he came to where the Brahman woman sat. Suddenly her bosom well nigh burst with joy; for marvellous to relate, she recognised, through Jivati's aid, her baby boy whom she had never seen in the prince who stood before her. When she told this to the prince, he became very angry and put down the pan of ghee and lay down in a corner and sulked. Every effort was made, but in vain, to appease his anger. At last the Queen went to him and told him the whole story. "People think I am your mother," said the Queen, "but I am not. She is your real mother." Then the prince recovered his good humour and the feast was resumed in all its former splendour. And he built for his real father and mother a big house close to the Royal Palace. And may Jivati be as kind to my readers and to me as she was to the Brahman woman when she helped her to recover her son.

X.

THE FIGHT AT KOREGAON.

JANUARY 1ST, 1818.

ON November 5th, 1817, Bajirao Raghunathrao, the last Peshwa of Poona, had definitely broken with the English, so long the friends of his father and himself. Weary of restraint and prompted by feelings of personal dislike to the resident he had launched the great army, gathered by him on the pretext of assisting the English in their campaign against the Pindaries, against the small garrison collected under Colonel Burr's orders at Kirkee. The opportunity had been eminently favourable. Fifty thousand British troops were locked up in Central India. General Smith, with the division, usually stationed near Poona, had recently marched to join them. The Courts of Shinde, Holkar and Nagpur were bitterly hostile to the growing power of the Company and a single victory would certainly have brought them to unite with Bajirao in a confideracy to destroy it. But the opportunity had not been profited by. The English force although out-numbered by ten to one had yet unflinchingly advanced to meet the enemy. The cavalry charge which was to have swept the foreigner from the Deccan had been hindered by a morass as fatal and unexpected as the sunken road at Ohain. And the

Maratha army foiled in its effort to gain a signal initial success had sullenly withdrawn into the Junnar hills. Here General Smith turning back from the road to Central India had followed it. The Peshwa, however, eluded his pursuer, and advanced on Poona wishing once again to try the fortune of war with his former enemy Colonel Burr. The latter had lost in the battle of Kirkee, eighty-six men, a serious loss to his small garrison. He, therefore, sent an urgent message for help to Sirur recently reinforced by a battalion of Indian infantry and a body of auxiliary horse.

On receipt of the message the 2nd battalion of the 1st Bombay Regiment, 500 strong, were detached; and with them at 8 p.m. on the 31st December, set out on a march as memorable as any in Indian History, 300 irregular horse and two sixpounder guns under Lieutenant Chisholm with a complement of English gunners. With the grenadiers were 4 English officers, Captains Staunton who led the entire force, Pattinson, the Adjutant and Lieutenants Conellan and Jones. The artillery was under Lieutenant Swanston and two Assistant Surgeons Wingate and Wyllie brought the number of English officers up to eight. The little force tramped through the long winter night and about 10 a.m. reached the high ground that overlooks the Bhima. Across its bed, almost dry in the cold weather their eyes fell on the imposing array of the main Maratha army. Bajirao advancing on Poona had heard of the near approach of Staunton's little force and had determined to intercept it. Its destruction would give him his long sought opportunity and, a thousand times magnified in importance, would convey to the great jaghirdars the welcome news of a Maratha victory and thus rouse them to join the Peshwa in warding off the growing English danger. Nor were his expectations unreasonable. Such odds as those between the opposing forces had never been heard of even in Indian history. The Peshwa's troops numbered 25,000 cavalry and 5,000 picked infantry. They were led by their prince in person. And although Holkar and Shinde, cowed by the grand army under Lord Hastings, remained inactive in Malwa there yet rode with Bajirao men who bore names renowned in Maratha history. Narsingrao Vinchurkar was there, whose fiery cavalry had just before Kirkee burst into the Residency, as Elphinstone with his escort crossed the Mula. Bapu Gokhale was there, the nephew of that Dhondupant Gokhale who had led a thousand horse in the 1st Mysore War and himself a man eminently brave, soldierlike and loyal. And conspicuous among a host of Brahmin officers was Ratnasinji, the great Maratha Sirdar of Malegaon. He claimed descent from that Shankaldev, who had been in vain betrothed to the daughter of Karanghelo, the last Rajput King of Gujerat, and who had lost both his life and his bride in battle against the Moguls. Nevertheless in spite of their numbers and the presence of these great nobles, the Maratha troops had but little spirit for fighting. The old Maval infantry which, led by Shivaji, had proved the equal of any in India, had been displaced by bands of mercenary Arabs, men brave indeed, but faithless, dissolute and averse from discipline. The cavalry, too, were chiefly new levies recruited ostensibly to join the English in the Pindari war. And officers and men alike mistrusted utterly the courage and the temper of the prince who led them.

On the other hand even though the irregular horse were not wholly trustworthy, the presence of 2 guns manned by 24 English gunners was of great value and the regiment of Indian infantry was a formidable fighting force. It was led by Captain Staunton, the bravest of the brave. The Adjutant Thomas Pattinson was a man of gigantic strength and stature and was worshipped by the corps he commanded. Half the rank-and-file were Musulmans recruited locally and embittered against the Peshwa's Government by centuries of political misfortune. The other half were Deccan and Konkan Mhars. They were drawn from the lowest stratum of society and oppressed and ill-treated from time immemorial by their more fortunate neighbours, had been welcomed as comrades in the Company's ranks. And on this day they discharged to the full their debt of gratitude. For they fought with the fierce courage of the French Huguenots under Ruvigny and of the Irish Brigade at Fontenoy.

Staunton at once grasped the situation. Advancing as if to ford the Bhima in the face of the enemy, he suddenly turned to the left and seized Koregaon, a little village on the river's eastern bank. It was surrounded by a low wall; and two temples of Bahiroba and Maruti to the West, and a large house to the North-West formed convenient towers from which to enfilade an attack from the river. And making the most of such materials as came to hand and with one gun guarding the Sirur road and the other facing the opposite bank Staunton's little band awaited the attack.

The ground precluded a cavalry charge, so a picked body of the Peshwa's infantry 1,800 strong advanced in three bodies to the assault. Two cannon and showers of rockets covered their approach. It was skilfully conducted. Staunton's attention was diverted by a feint from the Sirur road, while the main Arab force, carried the two temples which formed the chief outwork of the village. These were stormed at noon and further disasters followed quickly. Wingate, the assistant Surgeon, was stabbed to death. Swanston and Conellan lay severely wounded. Pattinson, the Adjutant, was shot through the body and fell as it seemed dead, while striving to retake the temples. Last of all the single gun, which, posted to the North of the village, had bravely answered the Peshwa's battery, was captured and Chisholm fell with 11 of the 24 English gunners. The troops who had not slept for 24 hours were wholly without water and provisions. It was thus no wonder that even the Englishmen engaged felt that honour had been fully satisfied and that the survivors might well ask for terms of surrender, while there was yet time. Nothing, however, could shake their commander's spirit. While he lived there would be no surrender. Nevertheless the position was one of imminent peril. The gun which alone had kept down the enemy's fire had gone and would shortly be turned at point-blank range against the defenders. The houses torn by the enemies' shells or lit by their rockets had become untenable and through the streets poured ever fresh bands of Arabs intoxicated with opium and flushed with success. But at this moment help came as it were from beyond the grave. Suddenly from among the heap of dead and wounded, rose Pattinson's gigantic form. Mortally stricken and left for dead his heroic spirit at this supreme crisis seemed to return to its earthly tenement. Once again his voice called his sepoys to the charge. The Mhars, who had idolized him, fancied that to save them he had returned from another world and followed him back joyfully to the assault. So inspired, it carried everything before it. In vain the Arabs refused to quit the captured gun. They were bayoneted as they stood. It was retaken, restored again to the surviving gunners and once more from its former spot it boomed forth unconquerable defiance. As the gun was recaptured, Pattinson received another wound and fell never to rise again. But through the whole of that afternoon the defence continued. Only four gunners and three English officers remained unwounded. But mercifully the short winter day closed in and with darkness the attack relaxed. The Peshwa's army weary with what seemed a hopeless task withdrew to the neighbouring hills and next morning learning of General Smith's rapid pursuit withdrew sullenly towards Poona. The following night the remains of the weary but unconquered force made their way back to Sirur.

Just six months later the Peshwa surrendered. The spirit of his army never recovered from its failure to destroy Staunton's battalion, and though surprised by General Smith at Ashta and beaten by Munro at Sholapur, its real victors were the gallant band, who, for 12 hours without food and water, held against the full military strength of the Peshwa's kingdom, the crumbling walls of Koregaon. Nor was the East India

Company grudging in its rewards. The 2nd Battalion of the 1st regiment were created, like the 1st Battalion had been for the defence of Mangular, grenadiers. They still bear the name of Koregaon in the regimental motto and celebrate with befitting revelry the immortal anniversary. But their leader Captain Staunton received exceptional distinction. On him were bestowed a purse of 500 guineas and a sword on which an inscription recited his memorable action. He was appointed honorary aide-de-camp to Lord Hastings and on reaching the rank of Major in 1823 was gazetted a Companion of the Most Honourable Order of the Bath. He did not long however enjoy his honours ; for on the 25th June, 1825, Lieutenant-Colonel Staunton, C.B., died at sea off the Cape of Good Hope. And Ocean received the mortal remains of one whose intrepid spirit no odds could daunt, no human enemy dismay.

To-day the little village of Koregaon sleeps peacefully as it did before Staunton's men sought its welcome refuse. Away to the West the foot hills of the Sahyadris dwindle to spurs and then to mounds until they pass into the rolling up-lands of the Desh—the country par excellence, the phile guia, the dear homeland of the Maratha. Far to the East, Sinhgad seems through the blue haze to look approval on the scene of a fiercer fight than any in its own bloodstained annals. The wall once so gallantly defended has disappeared, but Maruti's and Bahiroba's temples still stand. And a tomb half hidden by prickly pears may yet be traced which marks the spot where the gun stood and where its defenders ashes were laid to rest. Across the Bhima and facing the village stands superb in its lonely defiance a triumphal column. And it tells in words, that still stir the blood like a trumpet call, the tale how Staunton's 800 men held through the live long winter day Koregaon against the whole of the Peshwa's army!

The inscription on the monument runs as follows:—

This Column
is erected to commemorate the defence of Koregaum
by a Detachment commanded by Captain
Staunton of the Bombay Establishment,
which was surrounded on the 1st of January, 1818,
by the Peshwa's whole army under his
personal command
and withstood throughout the day a series of
the most obstinate
and sanguinary assaults of his best troops.
Captain Staunton,
under the most appalling circumstances,
persevered in his desperate resistance
and, seconded by the unconquerable spirit of
his Detachment,
at length achieved the signal discomfiture of
the Enemy
and accomplished one of the proudest
triumphs
of the British army in the East.

To perpetuate
the Memory of the brave troops
to whose heroic firmness and devotion it owes
the glory of that day,
the British Government
has directed the names of their Corps and of
the killed and wounded
to be inscribed on this monument.

XI

BAJIRAO II.

THE LAST PHASE.

THE last days of abdicated or deposed princes are as a rule neglected by the historian as beneath the dignity of the Muse of history. Nevertheless rulers have often after their retirement furnished material more entertaining and instructive than they ever did in the days of their power. The escapades of Queen Christina of Sweden were written large in the diplomatic records of half a dozen European courts. The dissipations of the last Bourbon king of Naples are said to have suggested to Daudet the character of King Rigolo in "Les rois en exil." The last days of Victor Amadeus of Savoy were hardly less tragic than the evil days of King Lear. It may, therefore, not be without interest to enquire what befell Bajirao II after he resigned on the 3rd June, 1818, to General Malcolm, the sceptre and diadem of Poona.

Bajirao II succeeded to the Peshwai after the death of his cousin Madhavrao II from the effects of a fall from an upper storey into the courtyard of the Shanwar palace. Through his father Raghunathrao, Bajirao II, was descended from Bajirao I and Balaji Visvanath. But his character and qualities were those of his mother Anandibai rather than those of the great founders of

13

the Poona dynasty. He was, indeed, handsome in appearance, fond of study and expert both as an archer and a horseman. But he was timid, treacherous and vacillating almost beyond belief. In 1803 he recovered his gadi with English help. In 1817 he quarrelled with his former allies and he conducted the quarrel so badly that within a few months he had neither home nor kingdom. On 3rd June 1818, he resigned to Sir John Malcolm all his sovereign rights and in return received a pension of £80,000 a year together with leave to retain his crown Jewels and to entertain a vast suite of officials, attendants and priests of whom a large number received further allowances varying from Rs. 6,000 to a few rupees a month. Bajirao II was allowed to choose his own place of residence. And when he had selected Brahmavarta or Bithur on the banks of the Ganges, the Company's Government bestowed the town on him as a jaghir. A beautiful site about six miles in circumference was assigned for the Peshwa's residence; and its boundaries were marked by sixteen stone pillars. The Company deputed a special resident to his court. The name of the resident was Captain John Lowe. He was thus by a curious coincidence the namesake of the officer appointed to guard the far more eminent exile, who since 1815 had been eating out his heart at St. Helena. But similarity between the lot of England's two distinguished prisoners ended with the names of their residents. At Longwood petty persecution, hateful surroundings, an incommodious residence, the society of an odious and narrow-minded jailor embittered the last days of the greatest of Europe's rulers. At Bithur the widest indulgence, an ample pension, a vast palace surrounded by a gigantic demesne and cooled by the breeze from India's mightiest river, consoled the last Peshwa for the loss of a power which he had never learnt properly to wield. It is no wonder, therefore, that the manners of the captives were differently affected by the methods of their captors. For six years Europe resounded with the complaints of the unfortunate Corsican. But so happily passed the years of the Brahmavarta exile that history, English and Indian alike, has entirely forgotten thc last part of his existence.

It must also be admitted that the characters of the two princes were responsible to a great extent for the different constancy with which they bore their captivity. It is possible that the easy going Bajirao would have resigned himself even to the rigours of Longwood. It is certain that Napoleon would have found but little solace in the pleasures of Bithur. Indeed it is probable that ample means, luxurious lodgings and abundant female society were all that was needed to complete the Brahman ruler's happiness. In Poona he had, no doubt, possessed them, but the fine which he had to pay was, probably to a mind like his, a heavy one. Protocols and despatches on matters of State were annoying interruptions to nautches and wrestling matches. At Brahmavarta the exile could exchange smiles with his dancing girls and jests with his court wits without the haunting fear that in the course of the next few minutes Mounstuart Elphinstone or General Wellesley might pray for an interview. Day after day glided by in a luxurious dream. On the Peshwa's palace-walls hung vast mirrors framed in gold which constantly reflected the rounded and charming forms of the most beautiful bayaderes in Asia. His tables groaned beneath their massive load of plate. His park swarmed with specimens of every kind of deer and wildfowl which India could then furnish. Singers, cithar players, jugglers strove with each other for the privilege of soothing the tedium of the most urbane of princes. Elephants and horses covered with gold lace and jewelled trappings were daily paraded past his door. And some 8,000 guardsmen, armed with every kind of useless weapon, recalled to the Peshwa the days when his generals could lead 30,000 men across the Moota river towards Kirkee.

But such was the curious mental stand-point of the Peshwa that, much although he loved pleasure, he loved religion still more. Bajirao experienced his keenest joy when he distributed gifts and alms to pious Brahmans. From the Deccan and Benares, from Allahabad and Gwalior, indeed from every spot which on one or another ground had a claim to sanctity poured into Brahmavarta a never failing stream of learned but poverty-stricken savants. At Brahmavarta, provided that they knew Sanskrit—for the deposed prince was an excellent scholar—they were certain of a gift and a welcome. And deeply attached as Bajirao was to the society of his dancing girls he was still more deeply attached to the married state. This oriental "super-Henry" married no less than six young ladies while at Poona and five more while at Bithur. His many marriages, however, did not bring the Peshwa what he desired most in the world, namely a son. One wife, it is true, namely, the Lady Waranshibai of the Phatak family, bore him a boy, but the child died within 15 or 20 days of its birth. His sixth wife, the Lady Saraswatibai of the Pendse family, bore him two daughters. One of these two, Bayabai by name, married a Chitpavan gentleman, the son of Sardar Babasaheb Apte of Gwalior. Marvellous to say, she is still alive and could no doubt relate to the curious a wealth of interesting experiences. When the Mutiny broke out, Sirdar Babasaheb was governor of the Gwalior territories in Rajputana. But although Sindia's troops went over to the mutineers, the Sirdar remained firm in his allegiance to the British Government. And for twenty-five years afterwards, he lived to enjoy the fruits of his good faith and loyalty. His son survived him for only two years. And from 1883 onwards the Lady Bayabai Apte has lived widowed and childless at the Durga Ghat of Benares. She has received from the Holkar Government a suitable pension. The British Government have made her a Sardar of the Deccan. And alone among all living persons she probably knows the exact truth about the Nana Sahib's end.

The Nana Sahib whose name was so long a byword in the British Isles was really given at his birth the name of Dhondu Pant. He was the son of one Madhavrao Narayan Bhat, a poor priest, who lived at Venegaon near the Bhor Ghat. In his book 'Under the Sun' Mr. Landon has written that the wife of Madhavrao Bhat was the sister of Bajirao's wife. But Mr. Landon has not mentioned to which of Bajirao's eleven wives she was related. However this may be, Bajirao II adopted Dhondu Pant on the 6th June 1827. And, extravagant in adoption as in everything else, Bajirao subsequently adopted in turn Dhondu Pant's two brothers Sadashivrao and Gangadharrao.

An existence similar to that led by Bajirao II wore out in a very few years the iron frame of Lucius Comelius Sulla. But so perfectly suited was the Peshwa's constitution to his life at Bithur, that he enjoyed the smiles of his mistresses and the pleasures of his table until the ripe age of 80. The researches of Rao Bahadur Parasnis, whose assistance in the preparation of this article I gratefully acknowledge, have unearthed a manuscript containing an account of the funeral obsequies of Bajirao II. It was written under the orders of one Raghunathrao Vinchurkar who was at the time on a visit to Brahmavarta and it contains the following graphic passage which I venture to translate as under :

"At the time of his (Bajirao's) death he must have been nearly 80 years of age. The news filled everyone with sorrow. Five thousand Brahmans and thousands of other people raised their voices aloud in grief. Hundreds of Brahman families, who realised that their daily gifts of bread had gone, began to fill their mouths with earth. All the shopkeepers of the town closed their shops and joined the wailing multitude. Altogether over 15,000 men gathered to lament the Peshwa's death. Afterwards the Nana Sahib carried fire in front of the corpse to the banks of the Ganges and there performed in a fitting manner the last rites. Then all bathed and threw sesamum into the water. Finally the mourners accompanied Nana Sahib to his palace and then dispersed. . . . . Next day Raghunathrao again went to the Ganges. There a large tent and a shamiana had been erected. . . .

After performing the necessary rites Nana Sahib took up some of the (Peshwa's) ashes and threw them into the Ganges. One after another all his companions did likewise until no more ashes remained. Then the mourners bathed, threw sesamum seed into the water and went home. On the 11th day Nana Sahib distributed gifts to the amount of 3 lakhs. But among the gifts there was none of land. Then Raghunathrao said to Nana Sahib: "The (Peshwa's) Government gave me two villages in inam. Beside these I own 50 villages in full sovereignty. If you wish, you can give any of these as a gift of land to the Brahmans. Nana Sahib made no answer. A few minutes later Raghunathrao repeated his offer. Then with tears in his eyes Nana Sahib said: 'I cannot answer you now. If you still care to do so, make your offer again next year at the memorial service. I can make the gift of land then.' In this way the rites of the eleventh day were completed. . . . On the 13th day Nana Sahib invited to dinner all those assembled. After dinner each one in turn made consolatory speeches. And Raghunathrao after a few suitable words obtained leave to return to the Deccan."

On Bajirao's death Dhondu Pant succeeded to his father's savings which amounted to £400,000 and to his sovereign rights over Bithur. The Company refused to continue to him his adoptive father's pension of £80,000 a year. It has often been supposed that enraged at this refusal, the Nana Sahib, dissembling his anger, waited until the chance came and then with devilish malice and forethought wreaked his vengeance on the Cawnpore garrison and their women and children. This view is probably mistaken. Bajirao II was at the close of his life a warm friend of the British. On one occasion he lent the Company six lakhs. During the Sikh War he equipped at his own expense two regiments—one of infantry and one of cavalry—for the Company's service. Dhondu Pant, therefore, did not start with any family prejudices against the English. The wording of his father's treaty with General Malcolm did, it is true, leave a loophole for Nana Sahib's claim that the pension should be continued. Nevertheless were any ordinary man to read the treaty, he would interpret it to mean that the Company conferred only a life pension on Bajirao. Dhondu Pant, therefore, must have foreseen the probable refusal of his demand. He was in no real need of money. And he would hardly have sought, as he did, English society, if he had not liked to meet and talk with English people. So far as one can judge, he was simply an ignorant ill-brought up boy who, like the Emperor Nero, was not naturally bad, but who had received from his parents no moral education and from Nature no moral stamina. A gradual misuse of power led the last Julian Emperor to the murder of his mother. A sudden access of power led Nana Sahib to the massacre of Cawnpore. Yet if the son of Agrippina had died within five years of Claudian's death, he would have left a character for clemency and moderation not inferior to that left by the Emperor Titus. If the son of Bajirao had died within six years of his father's death, he would have left the name of a kindly, courtly and hospitable country gentleman.

XII.

THE FORT OF LOHGAD.

FOR those of my readers who have not frequently crossed the Western Ghats, I should preface my remarks by saying that Lohgad is one of three great hills opposite to Karla, which run east to west more or less parallel with the Bombay-Poona Railway. The most easternly is called the Bhatrashi or Rice Heap from the close resemblance which its summit bears to the grain heaped in the threshing floor after the rice harvest has been gathered in. The middle and largest hill bears the name of Visapur and, as it is believed, was first fortified by Balaji Vishvanath, while the most westernly hill is styled Lohgad and is the subject of this article. I had long wished to see it and when duty brought me to Khandala, I took advantage of the chance offered. Starting early one October morning our party of two drove by tonga to where the road to the Karla caves branches from the main road to Poona, and then turning sharp by to the right crossed the Indrayani river and came to Karla station. There alighting we rode for two miles to the village of Bhaja and the foot of the hill we wished to scale.

Nothing of importance marked the earlier part of the ascent except the discovery and slaughter of an "ingli"* or black scorpion by one of the hillmen accom-

* The name Ingli comes from Ingal, a live coal, and suggests a most unpleasant result of its sting.

panying us. It was a monstrous beast as large as a cray fish and in size as far exceeded other scorpions which I had seen, as the heroes of Nestor's youth surpassed the degenerate companions of his age. The hillman in an awed whisper said that its single sting would have killed an elephant and I almost believed him! After half an hour's climb we reached the khind, or neck, out of which rise like two monstrous heads, the cliffs of Visapur and Lohgad. Turning to the right we pursued our way until just off the path we saw on a rough plinth no less than thirteen small horses in various stages of dilapidation. The story connected with them is an interesting one. It runs as follows: In the early days before the Bahmani Kingdom had arisen and before the power of Islam had penetrated the Deccan, six brothers came southward to convert its people. One of them was the great Sheikh Sallah of Poona over whose tomb the Sardar K. B. Pir Inam Zade still presides. Another brother was styled Bava Malang and he made his way to Kalyan, where he gave his name to a hill close by. A third brother was Sheikh Umar Avalia, the hero of my article. He had heard, it would seem, that a saintly Hindu devotee of Bahiroba lived on the summit of Lohgad and that his reputation for holiness interfered seriously with Shaikh Umar's missionary enterprises. The Mussalman resolved to remove his rival. He rode to the khind's summit and the horses mark the spot where he got off his steed and girt his loins for the task before him. First brandishing his spear he roared a warning to the Hindu to depart; and to give it force he drove his spear with such violence against the rock that it passed through to the other side, leaving a gigantic window visible to this day. Then Umarkhan began his ascent. But the path was rough and the day hot and by the time he reached the top, he was in a mood to kill a sanyasi as lightly as one might carve a chicken. Making his way to Bahiroba's temple he found the devotee in a state of beatific contemplation. "Sacrè cochon!" (or its Urdu equivalent) he bellowed, "did you not hear my warning?" But the Samadhi of an ascetic is not easily broken, so he heeded not the question. Then the infuriated Sheikh seized the Hindu like Daddy Long legs by the left leg, circled him like a hammer thrown by a Scotch athlete at a Highland gathering several times round his head and then hurled him with all his might in the direction furthest from the Kaaba and lo! the catapulted sanyasi—for such is the might with which Allah, the merciful endows the right arm of the True Believer—shot headlong into space. Passing swiftly over Lohgad fort and the khind leading to Visapur, he declined to descend on its hither bastion, but soaring like a cock pheasant over a Surrey cover he cleared two low hills in the centre of the fortress; then twisting like a well directed boomerang he turned northward in his aerial flight until he reached a small wood on the far side of the Visapur stronghold. There towering like a scuppered partridge, he rose to a vast height and finally fell a shapeless heap into the trees beneath. And lest a later generation should doubt the miracles of the Wonder Worker, a small Hindu temple marks to this day the exact spot where the crumpled Kafur alighted. Nor is other evidence lacking. At the summit of the hill and covered by a thatched roof is the tomb of the great Sheikh

Umar himself. And that incarnate Long Tom's descendants, who is in receipt of a Government grant of over Rs. 200 per annum, met us on the spot and he swore by the magic ring of King Solomon, by the purity of the 12 Imams and by the 99 names of the Most High, that the above story did not exceed by a single hair's breadth the strictest limits of the truth.

After recording this tale I am at liberty to consider the other history of the fort. From the Buddhist caves both at its foot and on its summit it was probably occupied by the votaries of that pacific faith about the third century before Christ. Indeed from their presence and from the resemblance in name and position, Lohgad has been supposed to be identical with Ptolemy's Olochaira. However that may be, Lohgad's real history can hardly be said to begin until A. D. 1485. In that year Malik Ahmed, afterwards founder of the Nizam Shahi dynasty, was first appointed as Bahmani, Governor of Daulatabad and Junnar. He was at the outset faced with a Maratha rising of which Sinhgad near Poona, and Lohgad were the principal centres and both of which withstood before their capture prolonged sieges. Having caused anxiety to the first King of Ahmednagar, Lohgad proved even more troublesome to his descendant, afterwards Burhan Nizam Shah II; for during four years (1590-1594) he was imprisoned within its uninviting perimeter. When we next hear of it, it is associated with Shivaji's first really overt act against the Bijapur Government. He had already made himself master of Sinhgad and Torna and had fortified Rajgadh, and the time was now ripe for more daring enterprises. Hearing that the Governor of

Kalyan was forwarding to court a convoy of treasure he openly attacked and intercepted it. At the same time by the traditional device of disguising his soldiers as grass cutters he seized no less than seven forts, of which Lohgad was the most important. In 1665, it was recovered by Jaising and Dilavarkhan at the treaty of Purandhar; but was recovered by Shivaji five years later, and remained until the fall of the Peshwa's empire, first a Maratha and then a Chitpawan possession. Indeed it is curiously connected with the rise of the latter dynasty. In 1713, Bahirav Pingle, the last Peshwa, not a member of the Bhat family, was sent by King Shahu to punish the rebel pirate Angria. Bahirav was so unfortunate as to be defeated and taken prisoner. And among the spoils Angria secured Lohgad. Balaji Vishvanath Bhat was then appointed by Shahu to repair the disaster. He succeeded so well that he recovered the lost fortress and got himself made Peshwa in Bahirav Pingle's place. The personage however with whom Lohgad is chiefly associated is the great regent Nana Phadnavis. He made himself master of it as early as 1770† by the help of a Koli outlaw Javji Bomble. The latter managed to plump a rocket into the middle of the magazine whereupon the terrified garrison surrendered. Nana Phadnavis seems to have retained possession of it through all the troublous minorities of Narain Rao and Madhavrao II. And at last, when as Bajirao II.'s minister he was rightly suspicious of his master he fixed on Lohgad as a possible

† This date is given on the authority of the Gazetteer, but I have many doubts as to its correctness. In 1770, Madhavrao I. was still alive and Nana Phadnavis had no power.

refuge. There he stored his treasures and there he resolved to hide if his master's treachery compelled his flight. The great statesman died in 1800, and his young widow, harassed by both Shinde and the Peshwa, was glad to seek in Lohgad the protection offered by her late husband's dependent Dhondupant. This faithful man protected his mistress for over three years and in 1803 actually fired on the Peshwa as he passed the fort. This brought about the intervention of General Wellesley to whose redoubtable arms Lohgad surrendered. But Napoleon's future conqueror fell shortly afterwards a victim to the young widow's charms. And in spite of her rebellious act she was, through the General's‡ intervention, handsomely pensioned by the Poona Government. General Wellesley restored Lohgad to Bajirao, but on the 4th March, 1818, it surrendered without resistance to Colonel Prother.

Knowing the Fort's close association with Nana Phadnavis, I sought for the great man's traces, and I was so fortunate as to find two inscriptions in which his name occurred. One was on the stone masonry of an empty tank and recorded that it had been built by Dhondu Ballal Nidsure under the orders of Balaji Janardhan Phadnavis, Nana's official designation. The remains of a bullock-run and a mot frame showed that it had been used for cultivation and may have helped to provide the garrison with fresh vegetables. It was, it is believed, drained in 1818 by the English, who

‡ General Wellesley described the lady as "very fair and very handsome, well deserving to be the object of a treaty." Her pension was fixed at Rs. 1,200 per annum.

vainly hoped to find treasure beneath its waters. My second discovery was a stone slab at the first or Ganesh Gate of the fortress which recorded that it had been built by the same Dhondu Ballal under Nana Phadnavis' orders and that the work begun in Shake 1711 Vaishakha Shudha 1st (April 1789), had been completed in Shake 1716 Jeshth Shudh 13th (June 1794). It did not, however, recall the ghastly history connected with the gate's foundation. Originally there was but the one gate known as the Maruti gate so called from a small image to the god on either side of it. But Nana Phadnavis added three others, the Ganesh, the Narayan and the Maha. The building of the Narayan and Maha gates presented no difficulty, but the foundation of the Ganesh bastion would not hold. Then Nana had a dream that the god of the hill must be placated by the lives of a man and woman. To get volunteers was not an easy task. However he at last induced a Maratha called Sabale to offer his eldest son and his son's wife. The unhappy pair were then buried alive. The god was placated and the bastion stands to this day. Readers will probably think that the minister paid a large blood price. Not a bit of it! He acquired without compensation the headship of Lohwadi from the Gadshi family and then conferred it with all graciousness on the Sabales who retain it to this day. Another victim of the hill was one Lomesh, the Rishi who lived there during the early Musalman times. He lived in one of the caves which honeycombs the hill's crest and when one of the Ahmednagar kings wished to interview him, he with his magic so confused the doors that it was impossible to discover the sage's room. After spending sixty bottles of oil in the fruitless quest, the king lost his temper. Exclaiming that if he could not find his way in the Rishi should not find his way out, he walled up all the entrances. The poor Rishi was never seen again and must have lamented sadly over the unfortunate limitations of the Black Art! The only other objects of interest in the fort are a broken temple to Maruti subsidized by Government and which I was petitioned—but declined—to rebuild at my own expense and a large Musalman tomb said falsely to be the tomb of Alamgir, but which may contain his queen's remains. But there is an amusing story about Lohgad to be found in Mr. Parasnis' "Court of the Younger Madhavrao." Sir Charles Malet, the English Resident at the Peshwa's court, had staying with him a painter called Mr. Wales, whose daughter Malet subsequently married. It was this gentleman's habit to go from place to place painting the forts and the personages of the Deccan. This did not, however, command itself always either to the authorities or to the villagers. The former had Mr. Wales followed by spies. The latter sometimes showed their disapproval in a more obvious manner. This may be gathered from an extract given by Mr. Parasnis from the report of Mahadji Chintaman, which I translate as follows:—

"Mr. Wales, the painter, was going from here to Bombay. On the way he made a painting of the Palegaon temple and went to Vehar. There he remained sketching until midday and then went to Bombay. I had written to you (*i. e.*, Nana Phadnavis) about this. But what do you think happened next? The painter, on reaching Bombay, sent from there a pupil and he also began to make sketches. Then the garrison of Lohgad heard of it and sending some men arrested the Topiwalla. They will neither take him to the fort nor will they send him to Poona. Therefore Bahirupant (the English Agent) has pressed me to beg you to order by letter the Lohgad garrison to release their prisoner."

As a matter of fact the budding painter was released. But one cannot help thinking that it was lucky for him that Nana Phadnavis had, by that time, finished the fortifications of Lohgad. Otherwise it is quite possible that he might have been transferred to the Public Works Department as valuable material for cementing foundations.

XIII.

A PICTURE GALLERY.

I

IT is probable that in all the Bombay Presidency there is no District Judge who dispenses justice amid such grandiose surroundings as the Judge of Satara. Graceful columns support the gigantic hall where former Maharajas held Darbars. Cool fountains mitigate the rigours of the hot wind and the asperities of pleaders' arguments. But most pleasing of all are the pictures which adorn the walls of the outer court-yard and illustrate the legends and sages of Vedic India. It must, however, be admitted that their presence is due to great good fortune. Students of history have often read of the Furia Francese and the Spanish Fury. But they were manifestations of mere nursery ill humour compared with the rage of a certain Indian Department, when it sees an ancient building. And this was never more clearly exemplified than in the present case. When, (to borrow a phrase from Macaulay) the "vile alguazils" of the said department first cast their fell eyes on the pictures in the outer court-yard, they at once sent for their terrible whitewash buckets. Flip! Flop! went the brushes in to the odious liquid. Squish! Squash! went the brushes on the painted walls. And in a few minutes the pictures were as if they had never been. Fortunately, the atrocity came to the ears of a beneficent Government. And these Indian Barberini were, by way of fitting punishment, ordered to have the pictures repainted as before by native artists.

The first picture portrays a monstrous animal riding on a no less monstrous bird. And in the corner, a giant, who has just emerged from a column, is engaged in tearing out the entrails of an unfortunate individual on his knee. The tale connected with the picture is a little lengthy. Once upon a time, four sons of Brahmadeo called Sanaka, Sanandan, Sanatan and Sanatkumara were strolling about the three worlds. They varied in age from two to five and consequently wore no clothes. In the course of their wanderings, they came to the door of Vaikuntha, the heaven of the god Vishnu. They told the chobdar and the bhaldar at the gate that they wished to enter. But the two attendants, after the manner of flunkeys, failed to realise the greatness of the visitors and told them that Vishnu did not receive visits from naked little boys. The four little gods lost their tempers. And they called down a terrible curse on the chobdar and the bhaldar. For three lives they were to lose their divine position and be born on earth as demons. And in due course, the two attendants were born on earth as Hiranyaksh and Hiranyakasipu, then as Ravan and Kumbhakarna, the enemies of Ramachandra and lastly as Shishupal and Vakradant whom Krisha slew. But, as Frankenstein found, it is one thing to create a monster and quite another to keep him in order. No sooner had Hiranyaksh reached manhood, then he revenged himself on the gods by dragging the earth down to the bottom of the sea. Vishnu, however, rose or rather sank to the occasion. Assuming the avatar of a boar, he plunged into the sea, slew Hiranyaksh and once more restored the earth to its former elevation. Hiranyakasipu learnt wisdom from his brother's fate. So before embarking on a sea of crime, he practised a series of stupendous austerities. Thereby he compelled the god Shiva to grant him a boon. The boon was that he should be killed neither by day nor night, neither inside nor outside a building nor by anything animate or inanimate. Feeling now reasonably safe, Hiranyakasipu started a career of unparalleled wickedness. He drove the gods out of all three worlds and ruled happy and unmolested for a million years. At last it really became about time to do some thing. And eventually Brahmadev's eldest son Naradmuni evolved a plan. When Hiranyakasipu's queen was about to give birth to a son, Naradmuni visited the demon's palace. Well received, he managed to instil into the unborn son of Hiranyakasipu an unalterable devotion to Vishnu. At the same time he bestowed on him the boon of immortality. When born the boy was named Prahlad and after a few years, his father handed him over to the care of a demon Guru called Shandamark. But, in a short time, the pedagogue sent back to his father the demon prince royal and complained that, whenever his (Shandamark's) back was turned, Prahlad induced all his fellow pupils to join him in the worship of Vishnu.

That his son should worship any god was bad enough, but that he should adore Vishnu, the slayer of Hiranyaksh, was more than Hiranyakasipu could bear. He began to torture Prahlad in every conceivable way. He hurled him from cliffs, dosed him with poison, flung thunder-bolts at his head, but all to no purpose, because of the immortality conferred on him by Naradmuni. At last Hiranyakasipu tried sarcasm. "Where, he asked, was this Vishnu whom Prahlad loved so much?" "He is everywhere," replied the much tried boy. "Is he in that pillar?" asked Hiranyakasipu pointing to a column in the palace hall. "Yes, he is" was the answer. "Then why does he not dare to come out?" sneered the demon king. The words had no sooner left his lips than the pillar burst asunder and Vishnu in a lion's form sprang out and rushed at Hiranyakasipu and now we return to the picture. The strange animal is the lion's form in which the god appeared. The bird which he is riding is the giant eagle Garud which habitually carries the god. And the small picture is an inset drawn to show how Vishnu tore Hiranyakasipu to pieces. For the boon given the latter by Shiva proved no protection. Vishnu carried Hiranyakasipu to the threshold, neither inside nor outside the building. There he drove into the demon's stomach the lion's claws, that were neither animate nor inanimate. And, as the time of Hiranyakasipu's death was twilight, it was neither day time nor night time. Prahlad, released from his father's tyranny, devoted himself with renewed fervour to the worship of Vishnu and in due course became the father of the celebrated Bali. The latter gave the gods almost as much trouble as his wicked grand-father had done. But, as Mr. Kipling used formerly to say, that is another story.

Let us now step a few paces on, until we come to a stout individual with an elephant's head. This is

Shiva's famous son Ganpati by the goddess Parvati. If ever an individual looked as if he had had a square meal, it is our friend so brightly depicted in red upon a white background. High upon the left is a little rat. For Ganpati uses a rat as his charger when he rides abroad. To his right and left are his two wives Riddhi and Siddhi ; and he holds in his four hands, a shell, a discus, a club and a water lily. There are many legends to account for his elephant's head. A common one is that his mother in her pride asked the god Shani or Saturn to look at the infant Ganpati. But Shani's glance brings misfortune to all on whom it falls and on this occasion it burnt poor Ganapati's head off. Parvati appealed to Brahmadev and he advised her to place on Ganpati's neck the head of the first animal which she met. It happened to be an elephant. With a turn of her wrist, Parvati dexterously snatched its head from the owner and placed it between Ganpati's shoulders. But elephant headed though he is, Ganpati has only one tusk. One day Parashrama, the Brahman avatar of Vishnu, came to Kailasa to visit Ganpati's father Shiva. But it was a hot afternoon and the mighty god was taking a siesta. Ganpati explained this courteously enough to the visitor. But Parashrama tried to force his way in. A terrific struggle ensued, Ganpati fastened his trunk round Parashrama and threw him to a great distance. But Parashrama returned to the charge and flung at Ganpati the sacred axe which Shiva himself had bestowed on him. Ganpati was too good a son to ward off his father's weapon. It stuck his right tusk with fearful force and chopped it clean off.

Ganpati is supposed to have written the entire Mahabharata at the dictation of the sage Vyas. And in consequence all books begin with an invocation to this incomparable littèrateur. The day sacred to him is the fourth of Bhadrapad known as Ganesh Chaturthi. On the night of that day you should not look at the moon. If you do some calamity will overtake you. Nevertheless you should not despair for Deccan ingenuity has found you a way out of your difficulty. Take a stone and throw it à la Pankhurst at your neighbour's window. Then bow your head reverently beneath the storm of abuse which he will shower on you. You are now free. For the expected calamity has fallen on you. "What about the neighbour" you will ask "whose window has been broken? "Nothing about him" is the answer. "Who is he that he should stand in the way of another's prosperity? How dare he ask for compensation? *Que le diable l'emporte* !"

XIV.

A PICTURE GALLERY.

II.

IN the closing part of my last article, I described Ganpaṭi. It is, therefore, only right that I should now pass over one or two intervening pictures and describe a portrait of his father. In the top left hand corner of the picture is a tiny white bull. Lower down but also on the left hand side is a gentleman standing with a pigtail trained to stand upon end as if it was waxed. On the right hand side is a gentleman with a horse's head. In the centre is the god Shiva himself. His hair is coiled so as to resemble a horn and from the horn flows a stream of water. In one of his four hands he holds the hind legs of a deer. On his right knee sits Ganpati, and on his left knee sits a young lady of engaging appearance. Below his seat is a tiger-skin from which a pair of eyes look upwards with a reproachful expression. Now let us examine these various symbols and ascertain their meaning.

The little white bull in the left hand top corner is Nandi or Nandikeshwar. This is Shiva's sacred steed upon which he rides when he wishes to take an airing. But the bull has other duties besides those of a charger. He is also the god's chamberlain and carries, as may be seen in the picture, a staff of office. He is also the official guardian of all quadrupeds. And, highly accomplished animal, he can play a dance tune when his master beguiles an idle hour by stepping the Tandwa measure. The gentleman with a rigid pig-tail is the sage Naradmuni. He is a son of Brahma, but he is best known as the agent provocateur of the gods. Whenever a sage has performed such austerities as to threaten the supremacy of the deities, Naradmuni is despatched to lead him astray. No artifice is too ingenious for him, no device too unscrupulous. But it is said of him by his admirers that if he does evil, he does it, like the legendary Jesuits, that good may follow. The gentleman on the right with the horse's head is the rishi Tumbaru.[1] But, as space is short, let us come at once to the great god himself. The coil of hair from which a stream flows is the source of the Ganges river. It came to be there in this way. A certain king Sagara of Ayodhya was so fortunate as to possess what might now be considered a large family, but what in those early days passed without attracting notice. By one wife alone he had 60,000 sons. With the help of his sons he so increased his kingdom, that he decided to hold an aswamedha or horse sacrifice. The rites of the sacrifice consisted in letting loose a horse and in following it with an army as it strayed. Any Government that seized the horse or resisted the army had to be overthrown. If the horse strayed unseized for a year, the owner declared himself emperor of the universe. Unfortunately the 60,000 sons had to deal with a superhuman enemy. For the god Krishna stole the horse, and when the 60,000 sons objected, he burnt them to

[1] Tumbaru is the leader of the gandharwas, heavenly musicians.

ashes. The duty now fell upon King Sagara's grandson Suman of making funeral offerings of water to his 60,000 uncles. But no river then flowing on the Earth had the necessary water supply. So Suman, and after him his son Dilip, and after him Dilip's son Bhagiratha performed tremendous austerities to bring down from heaven Ganges, the divine river which had its source in the god Vishnu's foot. At last the austerities were rewarded and down splashed the Ganges from the heavens. Had it fallen on earth, there would have been a deluge. So, to save all created things, the god Shiva caught the falling river and held it for a year among his matted hair. At last, helped by the further austerities of Bhagiratha, it found its way out and came to India. But by then all its torrent force had gone and it became the gentle, beneficent river that we know to-day.

Now let us consider the deer and the tiger-skin. The god ought also to wear a serpent round his neck. He does so in a companion picture elsewhere on the walls. Therefore let us suppose that he does so in this one. Once upon a time 10,000 rishis lived in the Taragam forest and had acquired such merit by their appalling austerities, that they threatened the supremacy of the gods. In fact the only way to save the divine dominion was somehow or other to steal away their merit. Shiva and Vishnu undertook to do so. Shiva disguised himself as a handsome young mendicant and Vishnu assumed the form of a beautiful young girl. They presented themselves at the rishis' hermitage and sought for and obtained hospitality. But soon disastrous results ensued. The rishis' wives fell in love with Shiva and the rishis themselves were all captivated by Vishnu. And, what with the wives being unable to resist Shiva's advances and what with Vishnu encouraging the advances of their husbands, the morals of the Taragam hermitage soon resembled those of the boarding house in Zola's Pot-Bouille. At last, the rishis perceived that they had lost the greater part of their merit. So they sent to Shiva a deputation. The deputation politely hinted that Shiva had outstayed his welcome and that the sooner he and his volatile young lady friend departed, the better the rishis would be pleased. The polite hint was entirely ignored. And next morning Shiva, in front of the hermitage, danced the Tandwa step with such elegance and precision, that not a rishi's wife there felt that she could deny him anything. The indignant rishis then took counsel together and "pooled" their remaining merit. They built a huge sacrificial fire and created from it a man-eating tiger. It sprang from the fire straight at Shiva. But the god without missing a step of the dance skinned the unfortunate man-eater alive. Ever since he has used the skin as a travelling rug. Then the rishis let loose a gigantic cobra. But the god flung it round his neck and has ever since worn it instead of a woollen muffler. Last of all the rishis created a savage black buck. But a god who had triumphed over a tiger and a cobra thought little of an antelope. He picked it up by the hind legs and regardless of its cramps and discomfort has held it so ever since. The unfortunate rishis had now exhausted all their merit. And they had no other role in prospect but that of *maris complaisants*. But since the rishis had been rendered harmless, the two gods had no further cause to stay in Taragam. They, therefore, departed to their respective heavens, leaving to the rishis and their wives the unpleasant task of mutual condonation.

I have already said all I have to say about Ganpati; so I shall confine myself to the attractive lady on Shiva's left knee. This is his wife. She is usually called Parvati. But Parvati means merely "she who dwells upon the mountains." Her real name was Aparna. And she and her two sisters Ekaparna and Ekapatala were the daughters of Himavat, King of Mountains. All three performed prodigious austerities. Ekaparna and Ekapatala ate only one leaf a day each. Aparna, however, was easily first. For she lived on nothing. So her distressed mother Mena begged her to desist and said "Uma" "O don't." So ever afterwards she was called Uma. Now Uma made up her mind to marry Shiva. In a former life, indeed, she had been his wife. She was then called Sati, but, on account of a quarrel between her husband and her father, she burnt herself alive. In this life, therefore, she determined to resume her former rank as queen of Kailasa. But it so happened that Shiva was tired of marriage and would have none of her. So Uma engaged in austerities compared with which her former efforts and those of her sisters were as nothing. But Shiva paid no heed to her and dreamed away the years in his mountain palace. At last Kamadev, the god of desire, took pity on Uma. He crept close to Shiva, intending to shoot at him an arrow that would have inflamed him with love for King Himavat's daughter. But Shiva detected him and with his terrible third eye he burnt Kamadev to ashes. Nevertheless, in the end Uma won her wish. Her ceaseless austerities at last induced the god to visit her. He disguised himself as a Brahman youth and tried to dissuade Uma from what he described as a hopeless passion and said all that he could to prejudice her against Shiva. But Uma, womanlike, defended her absent friend. And at last Shiva, convinced of her constancy and her affection, revealed himself to her and made her his wife. *Dieu propose et femme dispose.*

XV.

A PICTURE GALLERY.

III.

IMMEDIATELY to the right of Shiva's* picture is a portrait of a pleasant-looking person reclining on a couch. Below the couch is coiled a serpent whose six heads form a canopy over the pleasant-looking person's head. Beneath the serpent is a pool of milk-like liquid in which a number of fishes disport themselves. From the centre of the pleasant-looking person's body springs a plant on the top of which is seated a small gentleman with four heads. A young lady massages the pleasant-looking person's legs as he reclines on the couch. Round his neck and on his breast are wonderful jewels. And in his four hands are a shell, a chakra or quoit, a club and a lotus. This is a picture of the god Vishnu ; he is either the first or second of the Hindu triad, according to whether one is a Shaiva or a Vaishnava. The pool beneath his couch represents the Kshirsagar or ocean of milk. For Vishnu's home is in the ocean. And whatever part of the ocean he selects as his resting place turns at once to milk. The snake coiled beneath his couch and canopied above his head is the famous snake-god Vasuki. Now after the deluge, to which I shall refer in a later

* Shiva is never worshipped in the form of an image, but only in the sign of a linga. And in all India Brahmadev has only one temple.

article, everything that was of any value was drowned fathoms deep beneath the ocean. The earth, it is true, had emerged, but everything else that the gods prized, including their cask of Amrita or the drink that confers immortality, had been seized by the waters and they would not give up their prey. There was, however, one way to recover what had been lost. If the sea of milk could be churned into butter, then the lost articles could be recovered. Now in India a churn consists of a jar, inside which a stick is revolved backwards and forwards by means of a rope. So for a stick the gods tore up the Mandara mountain. For a rope they took the snake Vasuki. And, in order that the mountain might turn easily, Vishnu converted himself into a gigantic tortoise upon which the mountain revolved. But who was to pull the rope? To pull one end of it the entire body of deities were needed. This left no one to pull the other end. The gods therefore had to humble themselves and beg the help of their enemies the demons. They promised the demons that, if they would pull the other end of Vasuki, they should have half the Amrita which would be obtained by the churning.

The deluded demons accepted the offer. And then the gods proceeded to cheat them in a way which M. de Grammont would have envied. In the first place they stationed the demons near the head of Vasuki and he scorched them with his breath until they felt as dry as withered trees. Still the poor demons worked away at the churning hoping that, however much Vasuki might burn them, they would, in the end, be refreshed by a draught of Amrita. And in due course up came the cask of Amrita out of the ocean. And after it came Dhanwantarī, the physician of the gods and guardian of the Amrita cask. Next came Laxmi, the goddess of good fortune. Vishnu fell in love with her and married her, and she is the beautiful lady who in the picture is massaging Vishnu's feet. Next came Sura, the wine goddess. Next came the moon. Next came Rambha, a beautiful dancing girl. Next came the divine horse called Uchchaisravas. Next came the Kaustubha jewel which Vishnu took for his necklace. Next came Parijata, the tree that ever since has shaded the gods in heaven. Next came Surabhai, the cow that grants its owner all his wishes. Next came Airawata, the divine elephant. And this the god Indra took for a charger. Next came Shanka the shell. And this is the shell which in the picture Vishnu holds in his hand, for he uses it as a battle trumpet. Next came Dhanus or the bow. And last of all came a flood of Visha or black poison. This would have destroyed gods and men alike, but Shiva saved them by drinking it and his throat has ever since been a blue black colour. So he has been called Nil-kantha or blue-throat. When the churning was over, the poor demons thought that, as the gods had taken everything worth having they at least would give the demons the stipulated wage, namely half the Amrita cask. But Vishnu changed suddenly from a tortoise to a beautiful lady. The amorous demons rushed after her in a body. And by the time they had given up a hopeless chase, they returned to find that the gods had drunk every drop of Amrita. In vain the demons shewed fight. The Amrita had made the gods immortal, and they flung the demons into the outer darkness even as a hall-porter throws out an intruding stranger from a west-end club.

Now who is the four-headed individual on a plant? This is the god Brahmadev and the plant is a lotus. Originally according to the Hindus there was only one god or rather formless spirit called Brahmaj. From Brahma evolved Shiva and Vishnu and from Vishnu's navel sprang Brahmadev. And these three form the Hindu triad of to-day. But Brahmadev had originally five heads. He has only four now. For on one occasion Parwati for fun placed her hands over Shiva's eyes. But Shiva was in no humour or a frolic. He opened his terrible third eye and burnt up the Sun and the Earth, the mountains and all living things. And the flame caught one of Brahmadev's five heads, and it was consumed with the rest. At Parvati's intercession, Shiva restored the Sun and the Earth to their former state. But ever since, poor Brahmadev has had to manage with only four heads.

Last of all let us discourse about the wonderful jewels on Vishnu's neck and heart. That round his neck is the Kaustubha diamond which came up when ocean was churned. But on his breast is a still more gorgeous jewel. And it is called the Bhrigu-lanchan. Once upon a time there was a tremendous rishi called Bhrigu. And the other rishis, who were in some doubt as to who was the greatest among the gods, asked Bhrigu to decide for them. Bhrigu resolved to visit each of the three gods in turn and judge of them after a personal inspection. He first called upon Shiva. But Shiva was in his wife's apartments and the flunkey at the door told Bhrigu that his master was not at home. Bhrigu lost his temper and vowed that Shiva's image should never find a place in any temple. Bhrigu next visited Brahmadev. The sage, it is true, gained admittance into Brahmadev's palace. But the god showed him no attention at all. The irascible rishi pronounced that Brahmadev should never thereafter be worshipped by the Brahmans. He then made his way to Vaikunth to see Vishnu. The god was fast asleep, taking his siesta. The indignant Bhrigu at once kicked him in the chest. The god awoke. But instead of taking offence, he pressed the sage's foot and expressed himself honoured by his kick. Bhrigu's ill temper vanished. He returned to heaven and declared to the assembled rishis that Vishnu was the greatest god of all. And he bestowed on Vishnu the beautiful necklace that hangs upon his breast in the picture. It is so arranged as to cover the place where Bhrigu's foot struck the sleeping god. And so the jewel is called Bhrigu-lanchan or the kick of Bhrigu.

XVI.

A PICTURE GALLERY.

IV.

HAVING disposed of Vishnu, let us walk on until we reach a small alcove on the left hand side as one enters the palace courtyard. There will be seen two monsters with human bodies but with fishes' tails. One of the monsters is larger than the other and in his hand is a club. This represents Vishnu's first or Matsya (fish) incarnation. The smaller monster is the demon Haya-griya to whom Vishnu is dealing out strict club justice and this is the story connected with the picture.

Once upon a time there was a mighty rishi called Manu. Such was his amazing power of endurance that he stood on one leg, held his arms above his head and never once blinked his eyes for 10,000 weary years. Such a champion devotee deserved some special reward and in due course he received it. One day, as he stood on the banks of the Cherivi river, a small fish opened a conversation with him. Manu was naturally somewhat surprised, but with the courtesy which befits a rishi, he listened attentively to what the fish had to say. The fish explained that it was extremely small and that as fishes always preyed on those of their own species which were smaller than themselves, it was exposed to attack from practically every fish in the ocean. Manu recognised that life under these conditions had few attractions. So he took the fish out of the stream and placed it carefully in a water-jar. He daily fed it and it profited so much by its feeding that Manu took it out of the jar and placed it in a pond. But soon the pond became too narrow for the growing fish. So Manu carried it to the Ganges. But soon the fish outgrew even the sacred river, so the kindly Manu carried it to the ocean. Then the fish in return warned Manu that a deluge was about to come and that he should get an ark ready and that in it he should take refuge when the flood overwhelmed the earth. Advice given by a fish of these dimensions naturally carried some weight. And Manu worked hard until he had finished his ark. And then the prophesied deluge occurred. It happened in this way. One day the god Brahmadev overslept himself. The results were deplorable. Deprived of his control, the sea no longer remained within its borders but, rushed across the inhabited earth. Nor was this all. The demon Hayagriya, seizing the opportunity, stole the Vedas from the sleeping God and with them dived beneath the ocean. Manu, however, warned by the fish boarded his ark and headed for the open sea. But the weather, which he encountered, was terrible. The ark, to use the graphic phrase of Markandeya, reeled about like a drunken harlot. And it would probably have been lost had not the friendly fish again come to the rescue. This time a gigantic horn emerged from its head and, a miraculous cable appearing, Manu moored his ark to the fish's head. The fish then towed Manu towards one of the peaks of the Himalayas which was just visible above the ocean and, with the aforesaid cable, Manu hitched his ark to Kichinjanga and waited for better weather. The fish then disappeared beneath the ocean. For the fish was really Vishnu and having saved Manu, he had other work to do. Diving beneath the ocean he overtook Haya-griya. Then followed the scene depicted on the wall. Vishnu clubbed the demon senseless and recovered the Vedas. Shortly afterwards the God Brahma awoke and once more order was restored. The sea retreated within its borders. The miraculous cable, which was our old friend Vasuki, the serpent king, freed itself from both peak and vessel. The ark grounded. And Manu once more walked dryshod upon his native India.

Now let us retrace a few of our steps and we shall find ourselves in front of a picture of a boy balancing himself upon one of the hoods of a five-headed snake. The boy non-chalantly plays the flute. A gorgeous green and gold tree shades his head. The body of the snake upon which the boy stands is immersed in water. On each side of it are two or three young ladies "mit nodings on," or at least very little, and with tails like fishes. This represents Krishna's battle with the demon-snake Kaliya. And the following is the story concerning it. Krishna is the 8th incarnation of Vishnu. And some years ago I related in the *Times of India* how Vishnu took shape as the child of Vasudev and Devki, how Devki's wicked brother, King Kansa, strove to kill him and how Wasudev escaped with Krishna to the house of Nanda, the cow-herd, who lived at Gokula across the Yamuna. There Krishna grew to boyhood with his brother Balarama. When Krishna was seven years old, Nanda and the other villagers moved from Gokula to Vrindavana through fear of bands of wolves, which began to infest the neighbourhood. Near Vrindavana rose the mountain Govardhana. And at its foot flowed the Yamuna river. Lilies and lotuses grew on the Yamuna's bank or rested on her breast. Her course sometimes narrowed into wild gorges and sometimes widened into mighty lakes. And gorges and lakes with one exception were equally beautiful. The exception was the greatest of all the lakes which lay at some distance from Govardhana. It was some time before Krishna and Balarama discovered it. But as they grew older they strayed further afield and one day they came to it. It stretched away further than the eye could see. Above it hung heavy clouds. And to its banks clung wreaths of poisonous vapour, that rose from its waters. On enquiry Krishna learnt that the demon serpent Kaliya had taken refuge in this lake. Formerly he had lived in the heart of the ocean. But through fear of Vishnu's eagle Garud, Kaliya had fled from the ocean and had hidden in one of Yamuna's lakes. On learning this, Krishna did not hesitate a moment. He climbed up a Kadamba tree that grew upon the bank of the lake and dived into it head first. He stayed under the water so long that Balarama ran home and told Nanda and his wife Yashoda that Krishna was drowned. Nanda and Yashoda came back with Balarama to the edge of the great lake. And there Balarama called to his brother.

In the meantime, however, Krishna, after a sharp struggle with Kaliya, had got the better of the demon serpent. And as Balarama called, Krishna rose above the surface and began to dance upon Kaliya's five heads, until he and his wives begged for mercy. And this is the scene which the picture describes. The green and gold tree is the Kadamba tree from which Krishna dived. He is playing on the flute to make music for his dancing and the fish-tailed decolletèes are Kaliya's wives. When Kaliya and his wives begged for mercy, Krishna made him go back to the ocean. Kaliya pleaded that if he did so, Vishnu's eagle Garud would devour him. But Krishna promised Kaliya that he would be safe. For when Garud saw the foot-marks of Krishna's feet upon Kaliya's head, Garud would spare him. And Kaliya returned with his wives to the ocean and there he has ever since lived in safety protected by Krishna's footmarks.

XVII.

A PICTURE GALLERY.

V.

WE have now seen all the pictures in the Courtyard of the palace. Let us, therefore, examine those in the porch. On the left hand side, as one goes out, is a beautiful young lady who acts as mahout to an elephant which holds in its trunk a garland. In front of her is an unfortunate fish tied to the top of a pole and 'comble de malheurs,' he carries an arrow sticking through his eye. A little further on is a well set up young gentleman with a bow in his hand. In front of him is a bucket of small bath full of water or some similar liquid into which he seems to be earnestly gazing.

This is the famous swayamvara or contest of the Pandawas in which Arjuna won the hand of Draupadi for himself and his four brothers. It came about in this way. The uncle of Arjuna and his four brothers was Dritarashtra. Now Dritarashtra was the direct heir to the kingdom of the Bharatas who reigned at Hastinapura near Delhi. But he was born blind. So his younger brother Pandu succeeded to the throne in Dritarashtra's place. Now Pandu, as because a Kshatriya prince, was fond of hunting. But although a good sportsman he appears to have been a bad shot. For on one occasion he shot a Brahman in mistake for a deer.

The indignant Brahman cursed him and shortly afterwards poor Pandu died. Then, blind though he was, Dritarashtra ascended the throne and the succession between his sons and those of Pandu became complicated. A modern lawyer would probably elect for the eldest son of Dritarashtra. For Dritarashtra was both the eldest and the reigning prince. As a matter of fact Dritarashtra nominated as his heir Yudisthira, the eldest son of the deceased Pandu. But shortly afterwards he induced Yudisthira and his brothers to go and live at Varanavata. There a beautiful house all of lac had been prepared for them. But they noticed with some misgivings that its walls, roof and the furniture inside it were all of highly inflammable material. And they had the wisdom to suspect that their uncle and cousins had formed the charitable design of roasting them alive. Their misgivings were confirmed by the fact that directly they entered the palace a guard was placed at the gate. They, however, frustrated their relatives' design by digging a subterranean passage through the floor of the house and into the jungle. And through it they escaped before their enemies, who were waiting for a moonless night, had decided to apply a match to the building. The five brothers then disguised themselves as Brahmans and made their way to Panchala where King Drupada was holding a swayamvara in order to marry his daughter Draupadi. When they reached the arena, they found it crowded with all the youthful princes and all the beauty and fashion of the neighbourhood. But the test by which Draupadi's husband was to be selected was no easy one. The competitors had to shoot an arrow through a ring at a fish's eye. The fish was suspended above their heads. But they were not to look at it. They had to make their aim by looking at the fish's reflection in a tub of oil beneath their feet. Several of the competitors stepped forward but, one after the other, they were at once excluded. So far from being able to hit the fish, they could not even bend the bow. So the judges told them that they could retire from the competition.

Then a competitor called Karna stepped forward. And this is the story of Karna. Queen Kunti, afterwards the wife of King Pandu and mother of Yudhisthira, Bhima and Arjuna was, when a growing girl and yet unmarried, so unfortunate as to fall in love with the Sun-god. One morning she was sitting by her window and she saw the Sun rise more beautiful than ever. And sitting inside the radiant disk she saw or fancied she saw the figure of the Sun-god himself clad in golden armour. The naughty little girl completely lost her head and unable any longer to control her feelings, she began to call him to her side by repeating a string of perfectly irresistible mantras. Suddenly the Sun-god appeared before her. Now it is one thing to be in love with the Sun-god and to invoke him when he is thousands of miles away. But it is quite another thing to see him unexpectedly at one's elbow in all his glory and splendour. The poor little princess was frightened out of her wits and begged him to go back where he had come from, ever so high up in the sky, like a good, dear, kind Sun-god. But the Sun-god was as hard as adamant and would not take his dismissal. "Young ladies," he said, "who invoke Immortals from the sky must pay the penalty." The poor little princess made what resistance she could. But she was very young and timid and, as I am afraid it must be admitted, very much in love with the beautiful Sun-god. And since he would take no denial, the end of it all was that nine months afterwards Kunti became the mother of an extremely fine little boy. Now accidents will happen even in the best regulated families. But, when they do, they should be remedied without delay. So Kunti and her nurse put the poor little boy into a waterproof basket and sent it and its contents floating down the Aswa river. The basket floated down the Aswa until it reached the Yamuna and then the Ganges. While it floated down the Ganges it was washed towards the bank. And there it was seen by the wife of one Adhiratha of the Suta or charioteer caste. She dragged the basket ashore, opened it and found inside the little baby boy as happy as possible. She took him out and adopted him as her own and called him Karna. And Karna grew up tall and strong and became the most famous archer except Arjuna in all Northern India. But every one thought that he was Adhiratha's son and he was known everywhere as Karna the Suta. When he entered the arena he took from the hands of the judges the bow and bent it easily. He would then no doubt have hit the fish but for Draupadi herself. The haughty young princess rose in her seat and said "I shall not marry a man of the Suta caste." So poor Karna had to throw down the bow and leave the arena laughing with vexation.

Then Arjuna stepped forward. He took the bow, bent it easily and made his aim by looking at the reflection of the fish in the oil tub. He then muttered to himself the Sanskrit equivalent of "Attrape Poisson" and let fly. The arrow flew through the ring and shot the unfortunate fish through the very centre of its pupil. And this is the scene delineated in the picture. Arjuna has just hit the mark and Draupadi has mounted an elephant, which is rushing to garland the victorious competitor. And here I wish I could end my tale by writing that Draupadi and Arjuna were married and lived happily ever afterwards. Unfortunately the facts are that when Arjuna took her home, she learnt that she was expected to marry not only him but his four brothers also. No wonder if the young princess felt some maidenly hesitation! Nevertheless she overcame her reluctance and in the end proved herself a good wife to her quintuple husband.

Now let us turn our backs on the much married Draupadi and look at the picture on the wall opposite. Here, too, an elephant mounted by a young lady is rushing up with a garland in its trunk. A small, dark individual is flying about with a bow in his hand. And a ten headed gentleman is struggling on the ground with a bow across his chest. This is the swayamvara of Sita. Sita was known as the daughter of Janaka, King of Mithila. But there was some little mystery about her birth also. For the king found her one day in a furrow, as he was ploughing his fields. But whoever she was, King Janaka adopted her as his and declared that no one should marry her unless he could bend a certain bow which had come down to King Janaka from his ancestors. If the bow which Arjuna bent required some handling, King Janaka's bow was far worse. For merely to drag it to the arena, an eight-wheeled cart drawn by 5,000 thousand coolies was needed. And this was not surprising, for it had originally belonged to the great god Shiva himself. But if the bow was even more tremendous than that of King Drupada the test imposed on Sita's lovers was not so severe. For it was sufficient to bend it to be a successful suitor. But the bow had an awkward quality of its own. If any one lifted it, in order to try for Sita's hand, the bow would hurl itself on the unfortunate competitor's chest and would trample his breast-bone until his friends carried him away. And this is just what has happened to the ten-headed individual in the picture. This was the famous King Ravana of Ceylon. Attracted by Sita's reputation for good looks, he had come all the way from Lanka, his capital, to try his luck at Mithila. But the bow kicked and trampled his chest and stomach with such effect that he had to be carried out of the ring. The little dark individual is an unflattering representation of Ramchandra, son of King Dasharatha of Ayodhya. He had no difficulty with the bow. He held it up and squeezed it in his left hand until it had not a kick left in it and then with his right hand he pulled the string with such force that the bow snapped across the middle. No wonder the elephant, which carried Sita, ran up with a garland of flowers, with which to decorate the incomparable archer.

We have now gone round the Court-yard and through the porch and have reached the outer door. We have thus exhausted our picture gallery. And I must bid good bye to the subject with the hope, that my five articles may at some future date prove useful to the traveller, who visits the Satara Court house. Unfortunately most visitors who enter by the outer door do so with a stout policeman on either hand. Such a situation is one which does not lend itself to a contemplation of the pictures which one passes. One's own concerns are of such immense and immediate interest. And the unsympathetic pair on either side care for none of these things but hurry one on so dreadfully. Let me therefore add the further hope, that, if any one of my readers should go to see the Satara Court house, he will come there unattended by the men in blue and that he will be free to roam at will through the picture gallery with his body unguarded and his mind unperturbed.